PENTHOUSE

60 – 69

50 – 59

40 – 49

30 – 39

view from the top

view from the top

GRAND APARTMENT LIVING

edited by Janelle McCulloch

images
Publishing

Reprinted in 2008
(The Images Publishing Group Reference Number: 772)

Published in Australia in 2008 by
The Images Publishing Group Pty Ltd
ABN 89 059 734 431
6 Bastow Place, Mulgrave, Victoria 3170, Australia
Tel: +61 3 9561 5544 Fax: +61 3 9561 4860
books@imagespublishing.com
www.imagespublishing.com

National Library of Australia Cataloguing-in-Publication entry:

McCulloch, Janelle.
View from the top.

ISBN 9781864702262 (hbk.).

1. Apartments – Pictorial works. 2. Interior decoration –
Pictorial works. 3. Interior architecture. I. Title.

728.314

Edited by Janelle McCulloch

Designed by The Graphic Image Studio Pty Ltd, Mulgrave, Australia
www.tgis.com.au

Digital production by Splitting Image Colour Studio Pty Ltd, Australia
Printed by Everbest Printing Co. Ltd, in Hong Kong/China

IMAGES has included on its website a page for special notices in relation to this
and its other publications. Please visit www.imagespublishing.com.

Additional photography credits: Matthew Mallet (pages 4&5,12&13);
Lisa Sacco (pages 11,200&201)

contents

introduction   10

box seat   14
DS Architecture

central park art   20
Gwathmey Siegel & Associates Architects

cream of the crop   26
Studio Gaia

duplex drama   32
Foley & Cox

duplex for a gentleman   38
Axis Mundi and Studio ST

fifth avenue   44
Gwathmey Siegel & Associates Architects

fine lines   48
Janson Goldstein

grey scale   54
Hariri & Hariri Architecture

haute couture on the harbor   60
Greg Natale Interior Design

high life   64
Wood Marsh and Mirvac

la dolce vita   70
Silvestri Architettura

la luxe   78
James Swan & Company

living large in london   84
Form Design Architecture

loft for a super hero   90
Resolution: 4 Architecture

manhattan transfer   98
Smith-Miller + Hawkinson Architects

miami glamor   104
Archiforma

new york, new york 110
Louise Braverman Architect

paris match 116
Alex Mony

paris perfect 122
Alex Mony

pure positano 128
lazzarini pickering architetti

roman holiday 136
Studio Transit

a sense of place 142
Alex Mony

simple luxuries 148
Claudio Silvestrin

sydney vista 156
Abode

terrace for two 164
aardvarchitecture

terrace theater 170
Studio Transit

tower spectacle 174
Rori Homes

venetian dreams 182
Filippa Gaggia

view to a thrill 190
Gwathmey Siegel & Associates Architects

window on the world 194
Resolution: 4 Architecture

index 202

social elevation

In 2006, New York, a city not normally known for superfluous adjectives and over-the-top responses, went into metropolitan meltdown over the listing of an apartment. The residence in question was the legendary triplex penthouse atop the famous Pierre Hotel on Fifth Avenue, formerly owned by publishing heiress Lady Fairfax and then hedge fund boss Martin Zweig. While arguments raged over dinner tables as to what was more well-known—the apartment, which, in its previous life as a 1930s ballroom had been the exclusive province of high society in Depression-era New York, or the Pierre Hotel itself, a grand, chateau-style building better known for its opulent décor and discreet service, there was no doubt in anyone's minds that the sale of the converted top floors would have made media headlines.

For a start, it had the ballroom: a grand, extravagantly scaled room of 3,500 square feet tucked under the gleaming copper mansard roof that was large enough to hold a Christmas party for half the city. Then there was the double staircase, made of Belgian marble; the five fireplaces; the seven bathrooms; the nine bedrooms; and the vast principal rooms … not to mention the rest of the 11,000-square-foot floor plan.

But most of all there were the views … 360-degree vistas that are so spectacular the makers of the movie *Meet Joe Black* cast the residence as Anthony Hopkin's character's penthouse in the film.

The place was, quite simply, the last word in apartment luxury. It was no wonder it caused renewed interest in this very glamorous style of living.

Penthouses and other palatial top-floor apartments have become some of the most iconic spaces in the world of residential architecture, particularly the aspirational kind. They speak of prestige, urban elegance, luxury living high in the sky, and of course a certain amount of social elevation. Heiresses, millionaires, media moguls, and movie stars have known of the exclusivity, mystery, sophistication, and symbolism of high-rise living for decades, but they are not the only ones who make up the growing market of luxury apartment dwellers. In the past decade or so, since the property and stock markets made instant millionaires of a certain percentage of the population (and hedge funds helped flush out the bank accounts of another percentage), these 'mansions in the sky' have become the preferred dwellings for all those who want to live at a more elevated level. They evoke visions of decadence and an enviable lifestyle, and because there can only be a limited number, set atop each rooftop, they are also reassuringly elite.

Ironically, when apartment houses first came to prominence, the top floors of buildings were considered 'lowly' and suitable only for servants and storage. The stairs to reach them made them unrealistic as principal residences, and so the wealthy opted for the first two floors, which usually had higher ceilings, grander moldings, and more lavishly scaled rooms. It was only when elevators were introduced that these previously out-of-reach areas caught the eye of investors, who contemplated the idea of living higher up, closer to the clouds, the fresh air, and the coveted views.

In 1925 one of the very first truly lavish penthouses was commissioned by heiress and socialite Marjorie Merriweather Post Hutton, who asked architects to design her an extraordinary 54-room triplex on New York's Fifth Avenue, featuring a silver room, a wine room, and cold storage for

her flowers and furs. She wanted the prestigious apartment to be a reflection of a full-sized New York townhouse, only on top of a tower. In fact, she only agreed to do it "if the builder would virtually recreate her house atop the apartment structure." The property, which was accessed by a private carriage driveway and a private elevator, featured a separate ground floor suite for a concierge and a complete suite of rooms for her parents. It was a whole new way of thinking in New York-style living.

In the next few years, some of the city's most eye-catching apartments were conceived and built on the roofs of the city's skyscrapers. Media baron William Randolph Hearst moved into a five-floor apartment with a triple-height hall in the Clarendon at 137 Riverside Drive. Mrs William K. Vanderbilt II resided in a 27-room triplex maisonette at 666 Park Avenue, while Arthur Brisbane stared out at Manhattan from a 20-foot-high, 70-foot-long living room in the Ritz Tower. Even Laurence Rockefeller opted for penthouse living, buying a Fifth Avenue triplex with 20 rooms, which is now owned by Rupert Murdoch.

A century after they came into fashion, penthouses and their luxury apartment counterparts have become the ultimate architectural expression of success, or at least inner urban living at its very best. They also offer some of the most extraordinary views in residential living.

While the majority of us don't have the funds to be able to afford a New York penthouse, or even one overlooking the rooftops of London, Paris, or Rome, there are still ways we can gain a rare insight into these luxurious homes.

The following pages offer a sneak peek inside the private spaces of some of the world's most magnificent apartment residences, and a rare glimpse into not only the designs of and lifestyles experienced in these palatial places but also their amazing vistas.

From edgy, sharply dressed apartments with front-row views of famous harbors to grand villas facing the waterfront in places like Venice and Monaco and of course eye-popping pied-à-terres and penthouses in the heart of Manhattan and London, *View From The Top* offers inspiration for architects, designers, and armchair viewers alike.

So come upstairs with us and admire the view.

Janelle McCulloch
Editor

box seat

New York, New York, USA
DS Architecture

Some apartments are just too beautiful for words. And almost too beautiful to live in. High above Manhattan, at the top of the French Second Empire-style Prasada building, one of the most prepossessing luxury apartment houses ever erected in the city, exists a graceful space that is glamor in its purest form. There is a whisper it was used in the film *Breakfast at Tiffany's* and you can easily believe it's true: the residence has the same exquisiteness as the rest of the movie; the same elegant Audrey Hepburnesque lines, and the same bewitching glimpses of the city. In fact, it is so spectacular, it is difficult to know what to look at first: the engaging vistas or the beguiling interior.

Owned by a family of eight from Chicago, who bought it to use as a New York pied-à-terre for their family and friends, the apartment was rather lifeless when they first moved in, although the elegant bones of the interior were still clearly evident. The owners commissioned architect Dara Schaefer of DS Architecture to do a rather hasty makeover six weeks after they closed on the property so that they could start using it as a private hotel of sorts. Rather than fit out the interior with pieces from Crate and Barrell, however, (one flippant suggestion), Schaefer persuaded the owners to go with something more fitting for an architectural gem such as this. Because the family didn't live in the apartment permanently, an all-white palette was chosen, which both emphasized the lines and detailing of the interior and acted as an elegant foil for the sweep of Central Park greenery that lies right outside. The result is a place that celebrates urban living at its best, a beautifully dressed pied-à-terre that's edgy but still elegant, carefully uncluttered, and beautifully pared down, and yet still with splashes of whimsy and wit. Very *Breakfast at Tiffanys* indeed.

The unifying theme of the residence is sophisticated simplicity. Each of the pieces of furniture that were chosen for the interior—all rounded up, remarkably, in one day—were selected for their purity of form. Each is beautiful in its own right, having been designed by masters of the craft, and each sits in harmony with the rest, and the residence as a whole. Schaefer was given carte blanche to furnish the principal rooms (the secondary rooms were given a simple white dressing), and ended up with two streamlined B&B Italian sofas, a scattering of classic Mies van der Rohe Barcelona chairs and ottomans (all in white), a striking Noguchi cocktail table, sexy Christian Liaigre benches covered in a marine vinyl that allows sticky fingerprints to be wiped right off, and white hides from Hermes Leather. Artwork was provided by sculptural lights, which light the intricate living room ceiling at night, and a chandelier in the dining room. The dining room table was chosen to reflect the rawness of the paneling, but also proved to contrast beautifully with the Christian Liaigre chairs, which reflected the geometric beauty of the 'cut out' walls, and indeed the city outside. Similarly, the Barcelona chairs also reflected the grid of the ceiling, both complementing each other—like a "Rothko next to a Cezanne," as Schaefer remarked.

It is a remarkable space in a remarkable building, distinguished by its quiet charm and architectural integrity.

According to author Andrew Alpern in his book *Luxury Apartment Houses of New York*, each of the apartments in the Prasada had, when they were first built, eight or ten rooms, with libraries, parlors, and dining rooms that could be reconfigured with 'sliding pocket doors'.

They also had fireplaces for grandeur (two in each apartment), and, for functionality, three bathrooms, two maid's rooms and a butler's pantry. They were designed to be grand spaces, and were further distinguished by a handsome exterior entrance that lead to a semi-circular loggia interior entrance. The waiting room, known as the Palm Room, was a barrel-vaulted, leaded glass skylight-enhanced space that boasted a stone fountain, marble benches, and potted palms. Alpern described it as "a rival of the public spaces of the finest of New York hotels, albeit on a smaller scale." The key to the Prasada, and to this apartment, is that both are quietly sublime in a way that only hits you when you move cautiously through the building, savoring every step. Elegant and also unexpectedly sexy in a New York way, both are a dramatic statement of what fine design can achieve with a little thought.

central park art

New York, New York, USA
Gwathmey Siegel &
Associates Architects

Of all the international cities with skyscrapers, it is perhaps New York that is most famous for its linear monuments to luxury living. The vertical nature of Manhattan has long been its most identifiable feature, and the one thing that defines both the city and many of its wealthier residents, who like the prestige that comes with residing high in the sky, right in the box seat for the glittering views. In fact, in some circles of New York, the higher you live, the better placed in society you are seen to be, perhaps because top-floor apartments evoke a certain sense of exclusivity, status, and privacy, not to mention a fabulously shimmering show of power.

But now, along with the height factor, there is a new social identifier for the rising class to worry about: space. Yes, the prestige of height is no longer enough to trump about. You need capacious living quarters too. Apartment living, it seems, has taken a whole different turn.

With an interior that is as grand as its vistas of Central Park, this lavish, 8000-square-foot Gwathmey Siegel-designed apartment has a scale that is breathtaking, even by New York standards. The apartment is within a single floor of a hotel building facing Central Park and the rooms are edged in fierce geometric lines, which perfectly suit the sharp horizontals of the city outside. Even without furniture, the empty space is a spectacular environmental sculpture in itself.

The owner, a collector of modern art, specified a program that included the integration of this art, and the result is a grand, gallery-like space that not only offers much-needed breathing room in a sometimes cramped metropolis but a place that is a perfect backdrop for his magnificent oversized paintings.

On a certain level, the apartment is the consummate summary of New York apartment living—a totally sculptural and architecturally articulate series of interconnected spaces with a major view orientation. But its greatest success is

that it integrates art with architecture in such a way that the aesthetics not only reflect and reinforce one another but also create a dialogue. Rather than simply being the surrounds; the walls that house the space, the architecture is the coequal frame for this art, along with the just as sculptural furniture, and the striking view. Every form, and there are many under the 8-foot, 4-inch ceilings, including a random matrix of columns and plumbing lines, is responsive to either the display of the art, the occupation of the objects, or the reference of the view. Even the asymmetries add to the incredibly serene environment.

Interestingly, it never once feels like a long, low, horizontal environment, thanks to the addition of an extended sectional modulation, which reinforces the sense of variation and disengages one from the perception of being in an overly flat space.

The material palette, which references a Cubist collage with wood, stone, integral plaster, stainless steel, and titanium, also enhances the mood of the apartment, and is integrated into the spatial hierarchy in a way that is both subtle and refined. The few carefully selected pieces of furniture are as sleek and streamlined as the rest of the space, and further add to the quiet luxury.

The highlight, however, is a private terrace with spectacular views of Central Park and its broad sweep of green and leaves. It's perfect for raising a martini to at the end of the day.

Photography: Scott Frances

In an age when architects are trying to define new ways of distinguishing penthouses and luxury apartments in a market that seems to be increasingly top-heavy with them, space, and the sophisticated use of it, is one way to do so. Gwathmey Siegel & Associates and the owners of this penthouse have proven that you can manipulate scale, form, color, and line in remarkable ways to create an ode to modern living.

cream of the crop

New York, New York, USA
Studio Gaia

If luxury could be defined by a single color, it would be the delicate shade of the inside of an oyster shell. Far more than white, piano-key black, Tiffany blue, or even the traditionally dignified charcoal gray, oyster and all its creamy similes reflect a level of luxury that just doesn't come from bold primaries or more raucous tones. It's the color of glamour. The ultimate contemporary expression of sophistication.

This private residence on the 71st floor of a building in Columbus Circle, New York, evokes an air of immediate refinement through its use of expanses of creamy oyster and oatmeal shades. To avoid blandness, which can happen with too many neutrals, it breaks the beige with differing levels and surprising textures and surfaces.

Designed by Studio Gaia, the penthouse covers two floors, the first 1000 squares; the second 875. The client's request was for a "place to dream in peace" as well as a space for creative thought. He wanted a palette of serene neutrals that eliminated visual stress while providing enough interest to inspire and entice. The materials chosen were deliberately selected to be quietly understated, and include cream Travertine marble for the living room flooring, cream plaster in a Fresco finish for the walls, pewter limestone for the kitchen walls and ceilings, teak wood for the powder room, and walnut tongue and groove for the stairs and flooring. In the living room, a wall the color of creamy satin is broken by fine keylines, which add to the geometric glamour reflected in the suspended candle-strewn light feature, the elongated dining table, the stretched mirror and the soaring fireplace chimney. The architecture is a coupling of refinement and cutting-edge design with an open-plan, loft-style principal living area that's linked to the second floor by a series of domino-like stairs jutting out from the wall. The kitchen, dining and living are all-in-one, making what could have been a cavernous space into a cosy, intimate interchange of living functions. The main part of the kitchen can be closed off with a pull of sleek gray drapes, leaving only the front bench as a slick bar—a clever move for when parties are planned. The sophisticated ambiance is further softened by the scattering of church candles on a striking chandelier, the modern box fireplace, and the twinkling lights of the city outside.

Upstairs, there is a sumptuous bedroom with more views of the city, a private sitting room or study, and a lavish bathroom.

But perhaps the most extravagant thing about this penthouse is the terrace. Terraces alone are rare in Manhattan, but when they are as big as the rest of the apartment, they are a truly luxurious addition. Screened on one side to enable a certain amount of privacy, the terrace is partly opened on the other to allow for the spectacular views. A dining suite, deckchairs, and outdoor benches invite guests to sit and take in the vista, while a lawn area gives it a feeling of Central Park on top of the city skyline.

Gorgeous, glamorous, and utterly seductive, it is a small penthouse, but, just like an oyster, it has grand ambitions.

Photography: Moon Lee

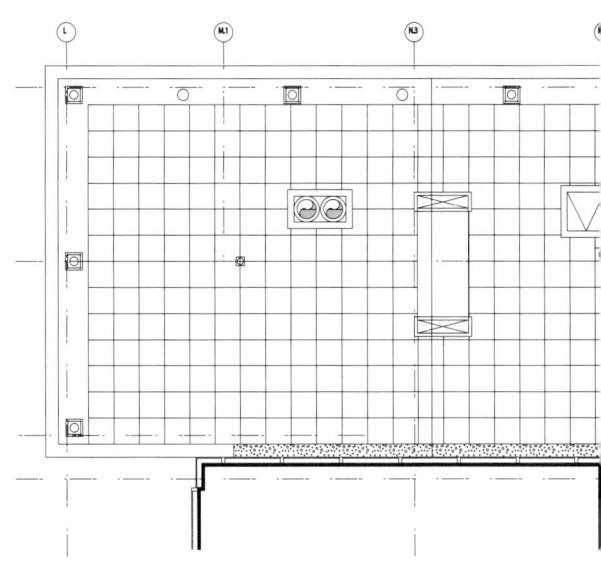

1   Living room/dining room
2   Kitchen
3   Powder room
4   Bedroom
5   Sunroom/dining
6   Bathroom
7   Sitting room
8   Terrace

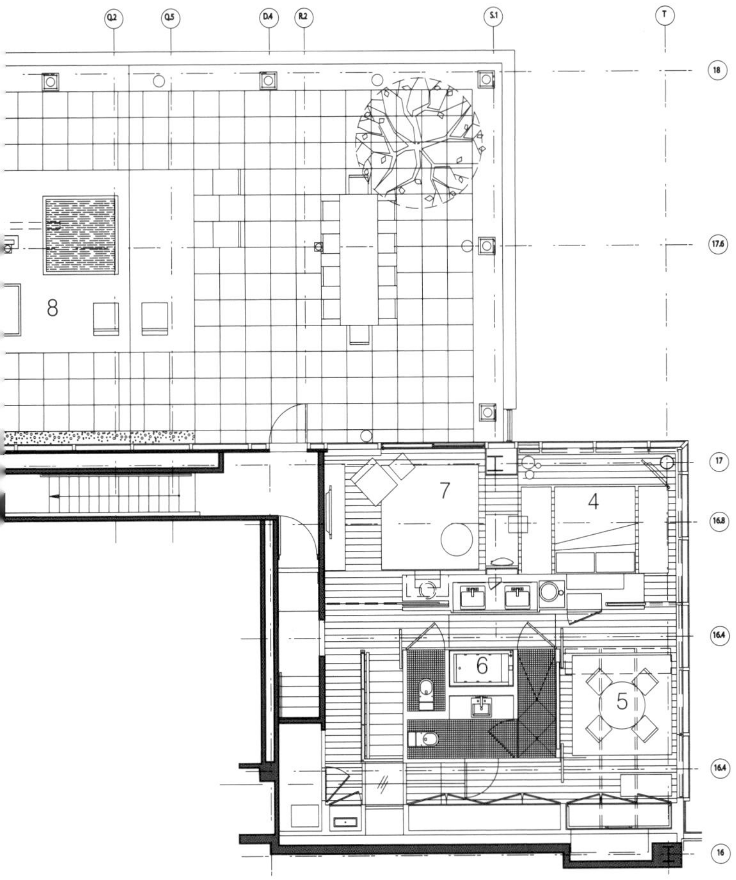

0   10ft

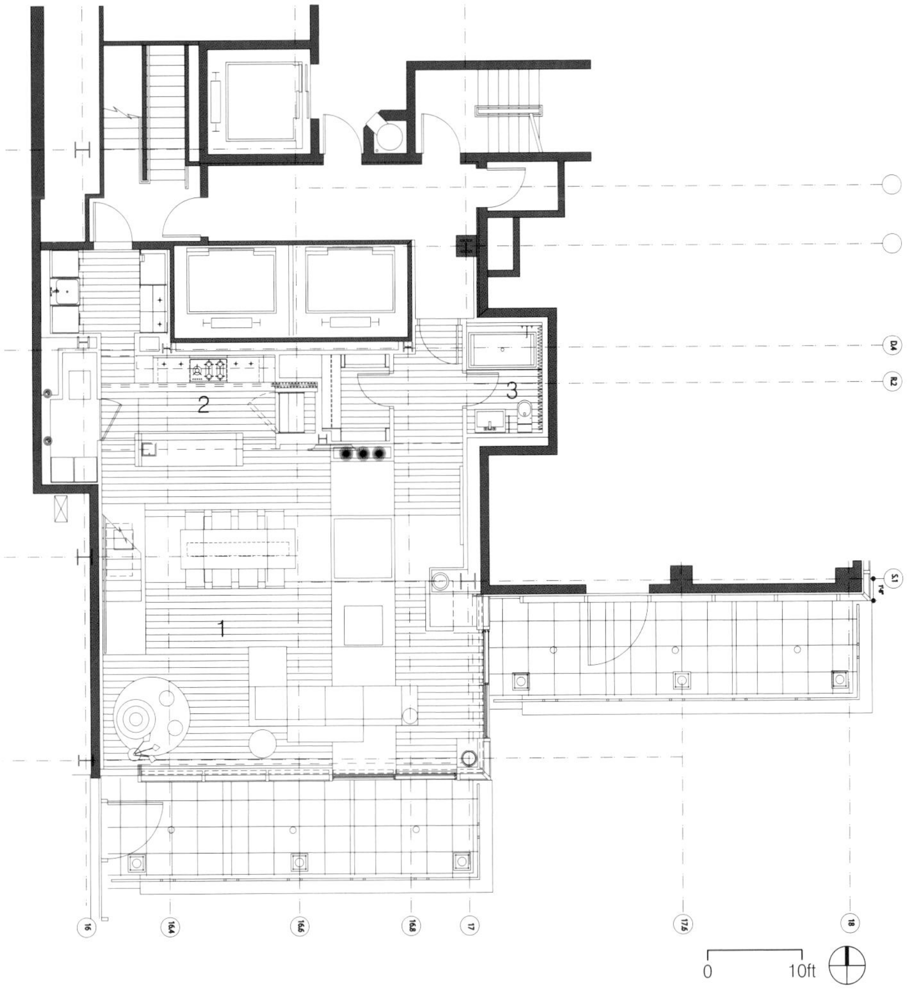

duplex drama

New York, New York, USA
Foley & Cox

There is something about the words 'New York penthouse' that makes you think of impeccably decorated abodes: the Cartier mansion, or the former home of Lady Fairfax in the Pierre Hotel, or the penthouse of penthouses—the triplex owned by William Parish in the film *Meet Joe Black*. For some reason, the words 'penthouse' and 'impeccable design' just go together, perhaps because the very mention of the former always inspires the latter.

For this reason, when it came to decorating a duplex penthouse on the city's Upper East Side with a spectacular terrace and a view over Carl Schurz Park, designers Mary Cox and Michael Foley of design firm Foley & Cox knew they had their work cut out for them. Especially when the terrace was used each year for lavish Memorial Day parties to kick off the summer season. To make matters more challenging, the owner and her family had lived in Malibu for years and were accustomed to brighter environments. The penthouse needed to be visually rich but it also needed to be light-filled and luminous, without being too LA.

Nevertheless, Cox and Foley weren't deterred. The pair is experienced in the penthouse look, having launched an interiors division for Ralph Lauren before starting their own business in 2002. They are adept at doing sophisticated but understated designs for over-the-top spaces.

With this duplex, they already had a head start in that the bones of the apartment were promising, and the scale and proportion of the rooms were right. They simply added a few subtle architectural embellishments, such as a new mantelpiece that emphasized the Art Deco design of the exterior, and ziggurat detail in the ceiling. And then they set about 'dressing' the interior.

To create more shimmer and shine inside, not to mention a Hollywood-sized dose of glamor, Foley & Cox added lustrous materials, fabrics, and finishes that reflected the light. The old palette of yellow, gold, and red was done away with and in its place a new, soothing neutral color scheme of silvers, beiges, whites, mushrooms, and platinums was introduced, which both opened up the interior and set the scene for the apartment's stylish new life. A glass chandelier was hung from the dining room ceiling, over the 1930s dining table, which immediately gave the space life, while wooden floors replaced carpeting, and zebra-print chairs in the living room provided a further wow-factor. On the terrace, chairs upholstered in platinum-colored cushions gave this already spectacular space a rich edge, while oyster-and-cream striped sofas beside the fireplace and a sumptuous amount of pannacotta-toned luxury in the bedroom, from vanilla walls to ice cream-white bed linen, created restful spaces high above the din of Manhattan.

While successfully creating a gorgeously glamorous, and fittingly luxurious penthouse space, the designers had to be careful that the new interior didn't interfere with the owner's collection of large-scale photography, which they did by keeping each of the rooms extremely 'composed.' Every piece, from furniture to fittings, was chosen with care, and rooms were pared down to the most beautiful essentials.

Now, apartment, artwork and interior meld together as one. It is a penthouse that has been cleverly dressed and accessorized, and the result is a beautifully turned-out space fit for both living and entertaining in style.

duplex for a gentleman

New York, New York, USA

Axis Mundi and Studio ST

Once, the epitome of the ultimate bachelor pad was a place modeled on a James Bond-style abode, or the luxury loft that Hugh Grant lolled about in the film *About A Boy*: a well-stocked library (books, DVDs, jazz CDs), an equally well-stocked drinks bar to create an elegant martini or whisky (plus top-of-the-line wine cooler), and acres of space perfectly fit for undisturbed social activities. Today, the modern man's private domain is very different, thanks to a new generation of architects and designers—and a new generation of men—who understand that interiors are far more than just a space to 'entertain'. They are stylish, private retreats to escape from the world, while looking out majestically over it.

Located near the distinguished Astor Place in New York City, this 2200-square-foot apartment was conceived as an 'apartment for a gentleman', and its masculine sophistication raises the bar of bachelor pads to a refined and almost inimitable height. The client, a 40-year-old bachelor involved in the film industry, wanted a space conducive to hosting parties, both grand and intimate, as well as a sanctuary from the bustling city below. The apartment's best assets were its views, which sweep across the north, west, and south, and take in the Empire State Building, the Chrysler Building, and the Hudson River, but the building's postwar design and plain rooms meant that these views weren't being taken full advantage of.

The designers, John Beckmann of Axis Mundi and Esther Sperber of Studio ST, set about creating a series of differentiated spaces, each with its own atmosphere and function, which together not only made up a coherent but flexible and easy living space but also embraced the inspirational skyline. The principal design element is a glass and metal conservatory, created by expanding the kitchen to the terrace, that blends inside and out, and features a fabulous hot-rolled steel TV wall—perfect for a man who needs to keep up with film and media industries—and Eero Saarinen table and chairs. Upstairs, on the second floor, there are further indulgence zones, including a magnificent master bath made from combining two closets, which features a white marble bath and a dark stained oak wood vanity with polished stainless steel fixtures. The dining room, meanwhile, is designed for dramatic dinner parties, with chocolate brown Venetian plaster walls and a large wenge wood table with 12 Mies van der Rohe Brno chairs.

Materials chosen in the interior design were selected to reflect the atmosphere of masculine sophistication: dark wenge wood for the linear, almost 'Miesian' entry wall and also the living room wet bar, walnut for the flooring, lavender Venetian plaster and panels of waxed steel for the walls, and handsome blue marble counters for the kitchen. There is also an Artemedie Nur light with Metamorfosi technology to provide the requisite 'bachelor pad' ambient lighting. The glamor element was provided by a plush, nightclub-style ruby red powder room, which offers a 'wow' factor for party guests.

The main conversation starter, however, is still undoubtedly the views. Here on the 19th and 20th floors, high above the metropolis, the vista is what really distinguishes this apartment from many others, and makes its owner feel on top of the world every time he comes home, no matter what kind of day he has had down below.

Photography: Andrew Garn

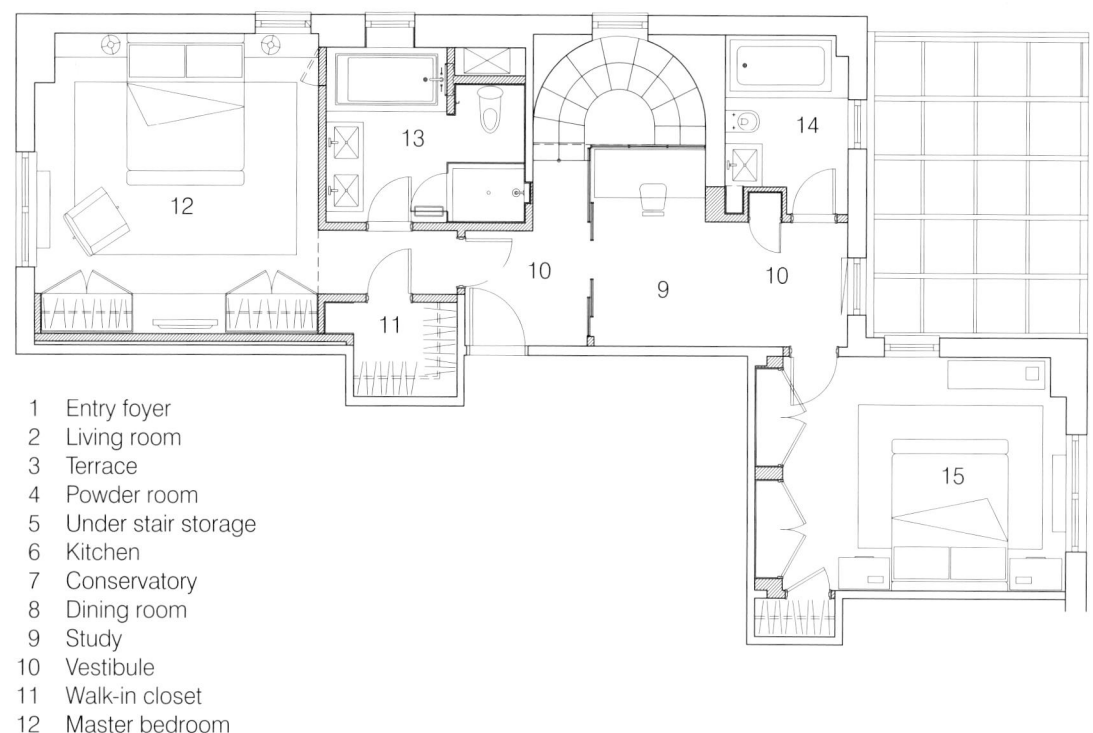

1 Entry foyer
2 Living room
3 Terrace
4 Powder room
5 Under stair storage
6 Kitchen
7 Conservatory
8 Dining room
9 Study
10 Vestibule
11 Walk-in closet
12 Master bedroom
13 Master bathroom
14 Guest bathroom
15 Bedroom

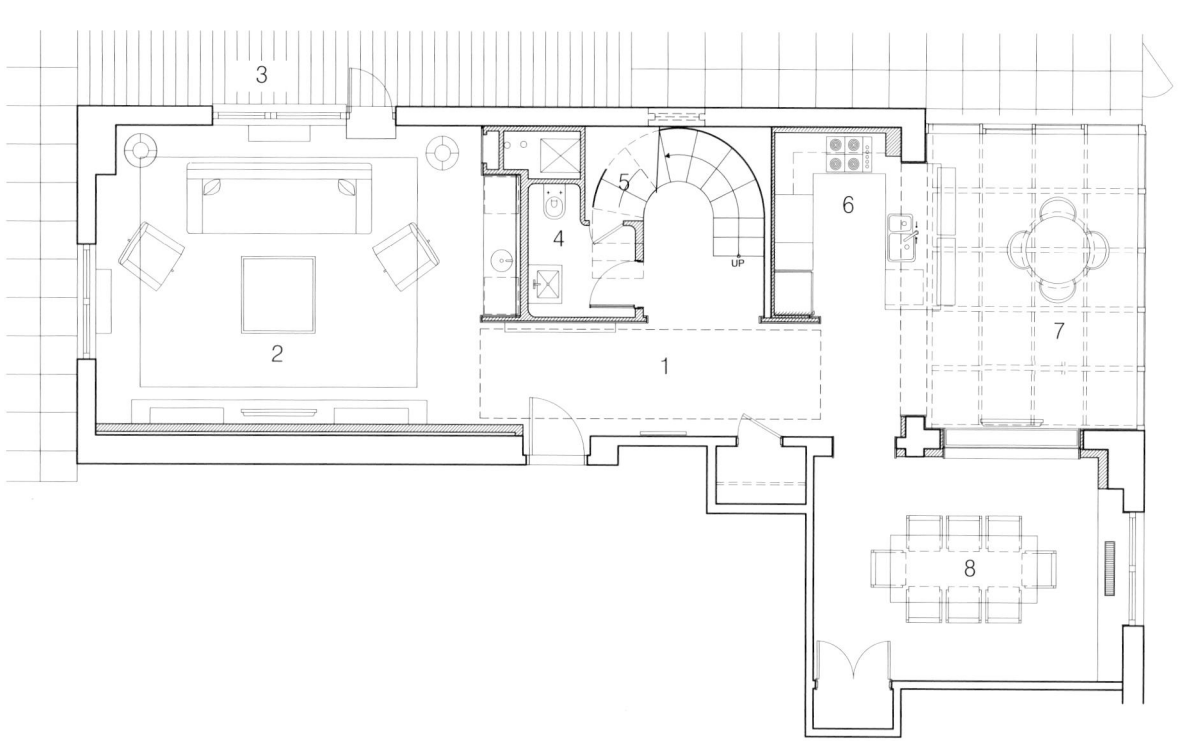

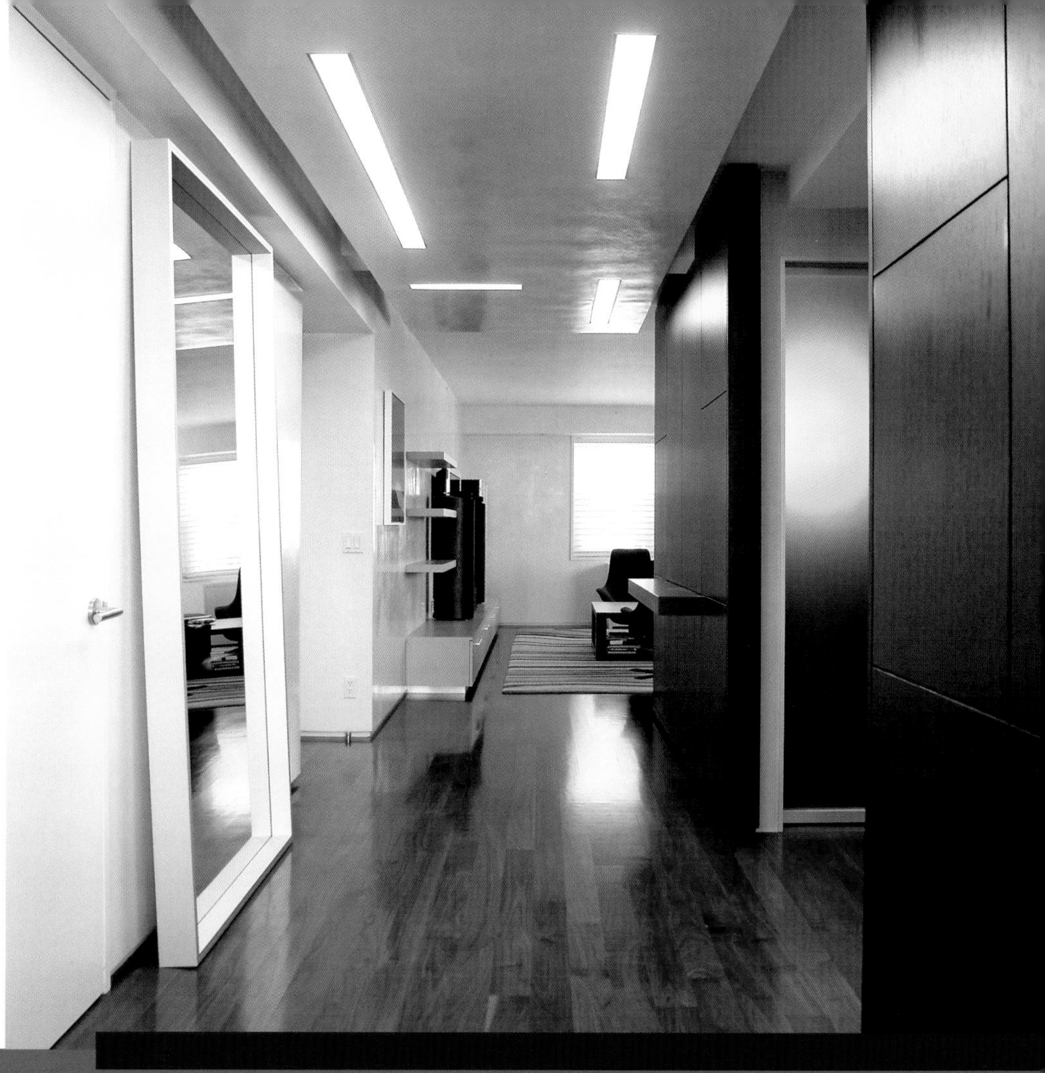
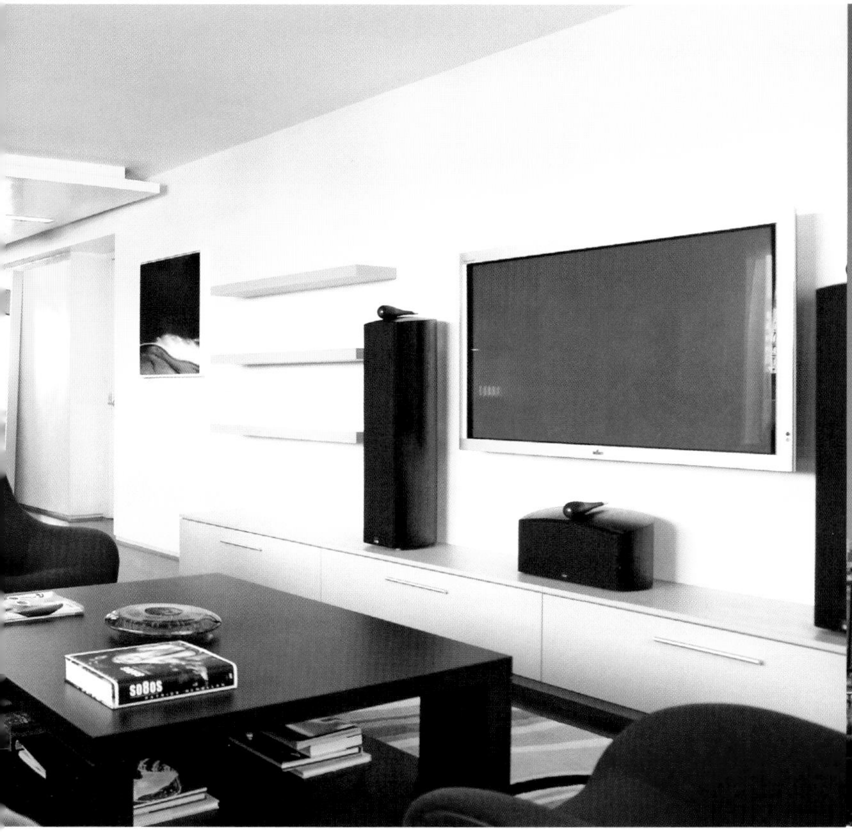
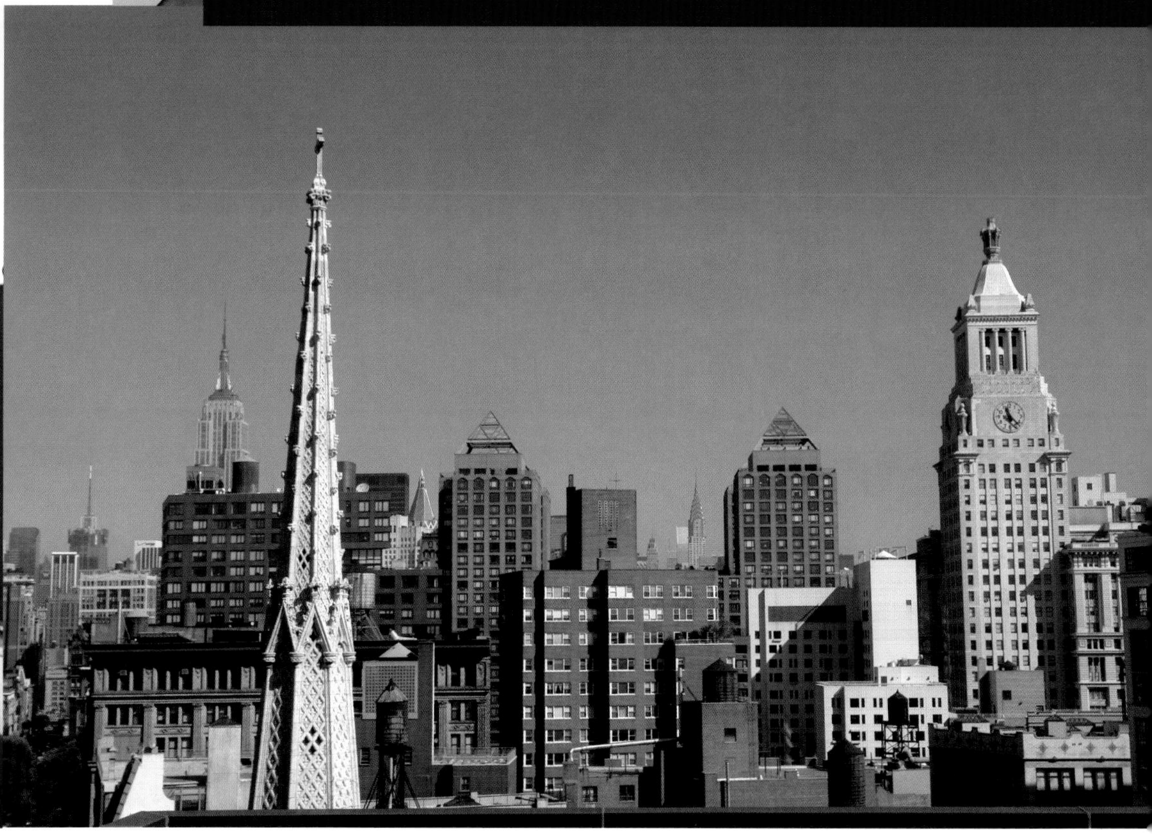

fifth avenue

New York, New York, USA

Gwathmey Siegel &
Associates Architects

This 2000-square-foot apartment is located in one of New York's most venerable residential hotels, on one of the city's most revered streets, at the southeast tip of the hallowed greenery of Central Park. This distinguished location, and the sheer prestige of it, meant that the architects needed to consider far more than just the space, the light, and the views when redesigning the residence. They needed to consider the 'grand' factor as well. It was no good designing an apartment that had minimalist tendencies, or indeed one that leaned toward the messy 'boho' aesthetic. Even if the owners had a strong creative side. The apartment needed to be impressive on many levels. It needed to be as majestic as its position.

The first thing Gwathmey Siegel & Associates did was to suggest a gut renovation in order to introduce spaces that were not only striking but were also notable for their formality. The idea was to create magnificent rooms for both entertaining and living that also had a kind of 'spatial serenity'—a challenge to do when the scale is on the imposing side. While the layout remained roughly the same, the entrance hall was opened up to create a vista from the front door to a window view looking north over the park, which served to provide a visual flow from inside to out. The ceiling heights were then varied to create interest, and plaster canopies and sloping and curving sections added for further effect. Custom cabinetry was also incorporated, some in deep cherry and others in a light steamed beech, to create streamlined storage within handsome façades. In some areas of the apartment, entire walls were covered in beech paneling, which lent a distinguished air to the already sophisticated interior. A brand new kitchen and dining area were devised to take the place of the old kitchen and a small bath, while a smart study/guest bedroom was designed where a second bedroom used to be.

Overall, the architects were careful to keep the apartment's interior to a classically formal style, which is sympathetic to the owners' collection of early 20th-century furniture. Additional layers of interest were added in things like textured fabrics and gray Swiss sandstone floors, which both emphasized the sense of lightness and reflect the layers of park and skyline views.

Gracious, grand, and truly memorable, it is an apartment that is now a perfect fit for its Fifth Avenue position.

fine lines

New York, New York, USA
Janson Goldstein

Head-turning views are nothing new in New York, where things catch the eye on an hourly basis. But this vista over Central Park from an apartment in Manhattan is enough to make even the most jaded of urbanites stop and look at again. It was certainly enough to capture the interest of its owner, a collector who wanted a pied-à-terre as well as a place to show her artwork and books. And you can see why she would want to buy. The view over the trees and the city is a sweeping one and is left unframed through bare windows unadorned by coverings—almost like a canvas that's too beautiful to surround by anything else.

The two-bedroom, two-and-a-half bathroom apartment was redesigned by New York firm Janson Goldstein, and tailored to fit the client's needs—and also her much-loved art. With a growing collection of photography, from Richard Avedon to Sally Mann, various paintings and even more design icons, the space needed to be clean, like a gallery, but also hospitable. Lighting is museum-grade, and walls are a quiet shade of off-white, but the rest is a place filled with personality and warmth.

Structurally, the place already had promise, but the architects added a few significant features, such as a round column in place of a square one to soften the hard-edged geometry of the apartment, and a curved wall in the foyer to draw guests in. They also opened up the space to encourage circulation and also allow for flexibility, as there is in a gallery.

As much as possible, they tried to keep the walls understated, so the owner could hang her art or display her books and design pieces. For example, the dining room has as its highlight nine portraits by the famous photographer Richard Avedon, which are hung in such a way that they seem like party guests. Other notable pieces, such as an Eero Saarinen Womb chair and ottoman and Tolomeo desk lamps look at home with art and design books piled in artfully arranged columns on the floor and photographs stacked up, gallery-like, on the side.

It is at once serene and intriguing, a marvelous, contemporary apartment that is both a show space and a place to come home to.

grey scale

New York, New York, USA
Hariri & Hariri
Architecture

If, in all their competitiveness, the real estate agents of New York ever came up with a way of putting a value on views, then the Empire State Building would surely come close to the top of the list. Vying with Central Park and the Statue of Liberty as Manhattan's most memorable landmarks, certainly at penthouse level, the Empire State Building is so iconic that views of it certainly add a significant amount to the value of any apartment with a direct perspective of its dazzling Art Deco lines.

This Fifth Avenue penthouse not only has a great line of sight to the Empire State, but also an impressive vista of the Washington Square Arch and the Hudson River. Inspired by the site, and the views of New York icons, the architects responsible for the revamp of the apartment decided to treat the space as a showcase of New York style. Part of this involved highlighting the various architectural elements that were prominent in the apartment, such as water and waste pipes—all of which are intrinsic to New York living. They treated the interior as an 'archeological site,' uncovering these previously hidden structures and exposing things like the original beams and columns as they did so. Polishing and dignifying these pipes and beams through a careful cleaning and restoration program, the architects celebrated their presence, and their significance in New York's living scheme, by displaying them in the open-space showcase of metal and glass. It was loft living, but without the sterility and starkness.

After removing many of the existing walls and fixtures and exposing the beams and colums, the architects then further opened up the apartment with a continuous limestone floor, which also invited the city elements to become a beautiful part of this new interior landscape. The outside venturing in, if you like. The inside was then brought out to meet the city via a spectacular wraparound terrace, which was perfectly positioned to offer a majestic view of the Empire State Building.

To add to the airy feel, a simple composition of planes and volumes was organized, which not only 'composed' the interior but also added to the sense of space and scale. A cantilevered plane in the dining area was created to offer a serving counter, a sculptural plane containing the central air conditioning ducts and the structural beams was built to make up the ceiling, while a series of planes that overlapped one another was formed to shape the base of the stairs, which connects the living area to the private, bedroom/library suite above. But perhaps the most striking plane is the library, in which pivoting bookshelves made of maple wood reveal and conceal the client's collection of rare and valuable books, while opening up and closing off the room, depending on the mood or time of day.

The apartment is now a poetic architectural composition of planes and volumes; simple but full of complex, interchangeable elements. It perfectly suits its owner, who wanted a quiet, contemplative, and monastic environment in which both he could live in harmony with his books, and with the city outside.

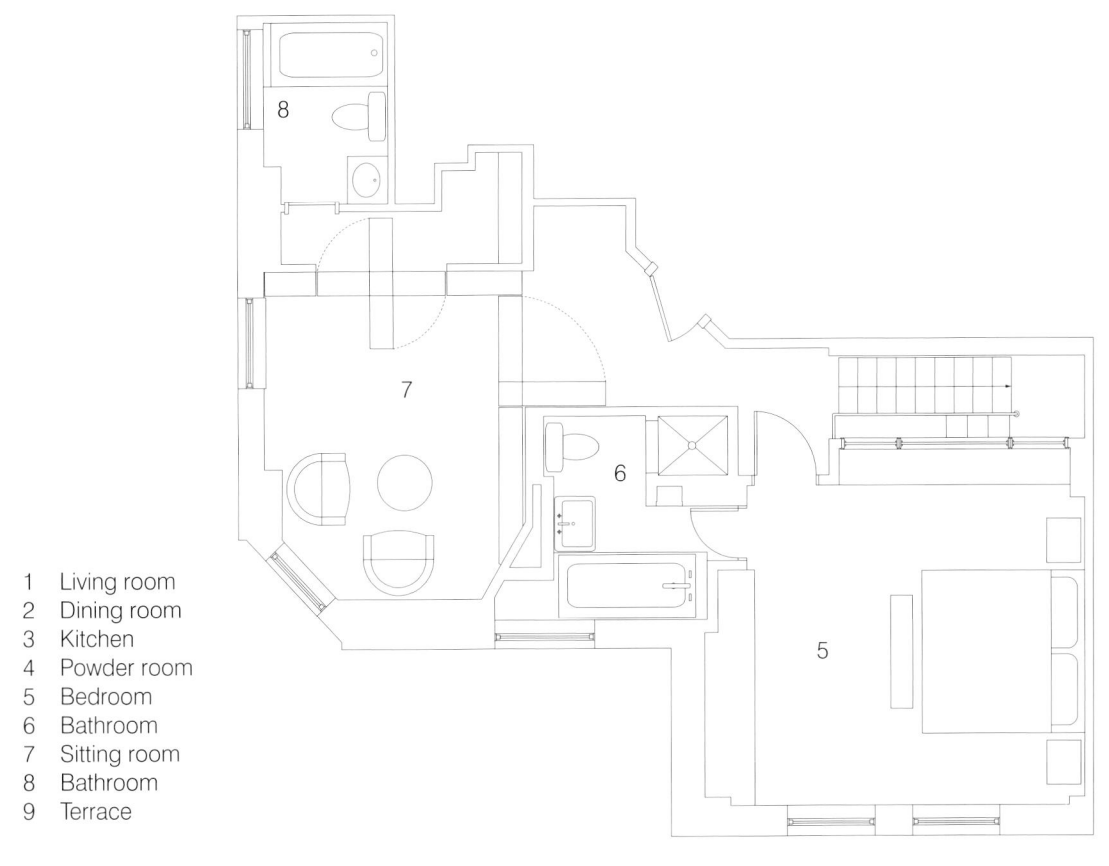

1 Living room
2 Dining room
3 Kitchen
4 Powder room
5 Bedroom
6 Bathroom
7 Sitting room
8 Bathroom
9 Terrace

0   6ft

haute couture on the harbor

Sydney, New South Wales, Australia

Greg Natale Interior Design

Sydney is a seriously sexy city anyway, with its glamorous harbor and famously dazzling Opera House, its ever-changing views of multi-million-dollar watercraft, and its gorgeous year-round weather. But when you add in architecture that screams chic (Sydney architecture tends to more extroverted than any other Australian city), the place turns into a veritable urban catwalk of non-stop drama and style.

The 'Samodol' apartment, designed by Greg Natale, reflects the city's modern sensibility and also its position as Australasia's most fashionable destination (according to Sydney, at least). The location, in The Cove, which is set on the waterfront in the very heart of the city, is as stylish as the view, which encompasses a flashy vista of the elegant bridge. But it is the interior when the glamour really shines. Here, the dark, moody color palette of charcoal grays feels very modern and quietly glamorous but still sets a suitably theatrical tone. It also comes into its own at night, when dusk turns the Sydney skyline a wistful shade of navy blue: somehow the gray palette serves as the perfect neutral 'frame' for the changing plays of light and tone outside, as harbor and horizon melt into each other in the night sky.

When everything turns to dark outside, however, there is still enough detail inside to keep residents and guests alike amused, including a richly veined black marble kitchen, subtly lit to provide an almost nightclub sense of drama.

The dining area, meanwhile, has a touch of Italian designer Missoni about it, with chairs covered in zigzag stripes setting the stage under a modern glass chandelier.

Elsewhere, the spectacle continues with a 'Priscilla pink' and gray bedroom suite and 'Dior gray' walls inviting more fashion references and inspiring more style.

Greg Natale's projects have been described as bold, exciting, dynamic, glamorous, sophisticated, having attitude, and bordering on kitsch—a bit like Sydney, really. But this apartment shows just how an ambitious collection of adjectives can work together to create a truly inspiring space.

Photography: Marek Lambert, Sharrin Ress

high life

Melbourne, Victoria, Australia
Wood Marsh and Mirvac

If there's one thing today's lifestyle pilgrims want, it's the perfect urbane abode to come home to; a place where they can retreat from the pressure of airport-hopping, indulge in a glass of good red or a freshly shucked oyster or 12, and watch the clouds drift by from 40 stories high. They also want a place that is fitted precisely to their needs; a bespoke abode that is custom-designed for their whims and desires in such a way, they need only to walk in the front door and the perfect CD begins to play.

The penthouse at Tower 5 in the Docklands precinct is tailor-made for such an aesthete. It is an haute couture space of the highest calibre, not only aesthetically, but geographically, positioned as it is at the very top of a landmark tower designed by Wood Marsh in conjunction with Mirvac Design to be an architectural statement in the fastest growing part of Melbourne. Both the apartment and its vista are what a globe-trotting connoisseur of fine living would expect: with near-360-degree views of the city, a sharply dressed interior courtesy of Kerry Phelan of Hecker Phelan Guthrie, and smart electronics that sense your arrival and adjust themselves accordingly. There are also enough modern and original pieces of furniture to open a gallery.

But the most remarkable thing about the T5 penthouse, which has been modeled on New York-style living, is the floor plan, which features ambitiously sized principal rooms, all with framed views of the vertical skyline. While not as grand as a house, these spaces are nevertheless extraordinary in that they are not only lavish in scale but reconfigure, depending on your mood, desire, or size of party, thanks to an interior wall that slides back. When closed, it cuts off the dining room and kitchen—which itself is a picture of glamour in dramatic, monochromatic tones—and when opened again, it turns the dining and living areas into a full-blown entertainment zone, big enough to satisfy even the most extravagant of party-throwers.

These aesthetic components are as integral to the apartment as the super impressive views. Mirvac, the company behind the project, realized that most buyers wanted a place that not only had a sense of space and superiority, and a prime position conveniently set in the center of everything, but also featured the same flexibility as a house. It's one thing to have an apartment you can lock up and leave when you fly off to Tuscany or Cannes; it's another to have one that allows you a certain freedom in your lifestyle when you're living there. This penthouse was designed to accommodate every need, from the personal (the ensuite is as luxurious as a day spa) to the social (the views will seduce any date, no matter how much of the world they've seen). It is so clever in its design that it picked up the 2005 Urban Development Institute of Australia Award and the Victorian Royal Australian Institute of Architects Award. A place for those who like to mix good looks with good sense, the T5 penthouse is pure theater for the aesthetically inclined.

la dolce vita

Rome, Italy
Silvestri Architettura

Overlooking Rome's famous Piazza Navona, this palatial apartment is owned by an Italian film director, and so its design had to not only befit a gentleman whose life is defined by the glamor and aesthetics of film, but be a flexible space that could accommodate both his public and his private lives. It had to be both a 'coffer' and a 'theater', while reflective of the owner's highly individual style.

Consequently, architect Roberto Silvestri spent a great deal of time talking with the client and musing over cinema, art, cooking, and books before he even considered the design. Working with these passions, Silvestri then set about creating a sensitive place that was rich but not overwhelming; strong but not harsh, cold, or uncomfortable.

Roberto Silvestri believes that it is impossible for people to live in geometrically perfect spaces and architecturally pure forms. He argues that it is better if private dwellings echo the same moods and even imperfections of their owners, for it is these things that gives them character. As a result, this Rome apartment is full of personality. The traditional house in which it sits is still visible, but the new interior is beautifully different, and a fitting reflection of both Rome and a film director with a love of life.

The access to the residence is from above, via a three-step stair made of Travertino Navona slabs. The rooms are not strictly connected, but at the same time, each separate space is still visible in the structure of the house: a plan that suits the contemporary way of Italian living. The living room is sparsely furnished: a pair of sofas, two small tables, a carpet, and a lamp, but the character of it is rich, thanks to a dark, velvety brown wall that adds a distinguished air. This is the first of two walls that are covered in Corten steel, usually used in exteriors. When adapted to interiors, it creates a wonderful dialogue with the floor and contrasts with the whiteness of the remaining walls.

The bedroom is similarly spare, almost monastically so, to serve as an elegant retreat from the excesses of the film industry, while the bathroom, by contrast, is a place for private luxury. This latter space has been created from enormous slabs of red marble that strongly contrast with the white of the walls.

Each of these rooms looks out to an expansive outdoor terrace, which, in turn, overlooks the rooftops and the Piazza Navona. It is a romantic space; a place to sip an espresso and look out onto Rome. It is also the exclamation mark in an apartment that fuses ancient and modern, bustling city and private retreat, and classic architecture and contemporary materials. In short, an apartment that is as spectacularly cinematic as its owner.

Photography: Ernesta Caviola, Roberto Silvestri, Million Matthieu

1 Living room
2 Sitting room
3 Bedroom
4 Kitchen/dining room
5 Bathroom
6 Terrace

0   2m

la luxe

Los Angeles, California, USA

James Swan & Company

The New York–Los Angeles dichotomy has long been a topic of debate at dinner party tables, with the issue of which boasts the better architecture—vertical versus horizontal—often continuing into the night. It's true that Los Angeles may not have the famed views of its east coast cousin, since its architecture is less orientated toward living in the clouds and more toward the sun. But it can still gloat about its many shimmering vistas.

This international-style high-rise focuses on two angles of the city's iconic skyline: the hills, the greenery, and the famous blue sky on one side, and skyscrapers and neon lights on another. Inside the apartment, the interior is just as reflective of LA's bold style: glamorous, fabulous, and not quite what you would expect.

Owned by interior designer James Swan, the residence was gutted, reconfigured, and rebuilt over an 11-month period, with the aim being to create a stylish collection of distinct living spaces oriented toward entertaining, whether on an intimate or large scale. As well, a growing collection of continental antiques and figurative art had to be integrated into this space without overcrowding it, while the color palette had to remain calming, so that the apartment became a serene home to return to after the madness of traffic and life in LA.

Fortunately, the apartment had classically proportioned rooms—good bones, as a Hollywood scout might say. So it was only a matter of emphasizing these lines and bringing up the beauty of the space.

The entrance now features handsome double walnut doors leading to a vestibule framed by steel and glass doors. To keep the classical theme, and to set the stage for the glamor ahead, the walls in this area are void of decoration or art save for scored plaster channels, which run horizontally in the spaces beyond, and a pair of painted plaster sconces. Past the entrance is an elongated space featuring a 19th-century gilded Italian mirror flanked by a black toile-painted torchére (with wax candles) and a pair of 18th-century English walnut tables. When the owner entertains, this section becomes a dramatic entrance for guests, who can then continue through to the right, to a small dining alcove anchored by an 18th-century Swedish corner bench upholstered in cream cotton. There is also a set of four Francis Elkin dining chairs here to provide a quiet graphic stroke next to an 18th-century Lyre-based walnut wine-tasting table from the Burgundy region of France.

It is in the living room, however, where the glamor quotient is really turned up. Against a distinguished palette, James Swan's sophisticated design skills have transformed the apartment into an urban playground, a rich gallery, and a serene city retreat in one. The collection of art and antiques include a pair of 19th-century gilded bronze candle-sconces, a pair of 17th-century Italian armchairs, and a quirky display of German architectural plans and elevations dating from 1772 that display the English alphabet. The kitchen is also fiercely chic—a study in black and white, it features lacquered cabinets and honed black granite counters and splashbacks. The study, meanwhile, features a brass cocktail table, and a black lacquer desk by the iconic French design firm Jansen, along with a large, eye-catching calligraphy screen. Finally, the master bedroom is dressed in a soothing shade of moss green and features green corduroy on the upholstered headboard and coverlet, and a Biedermeier desk. A collection of framed photographs of Rome from the late 19th century round out this refined Los Angeles retreat.

Photography: Erhard Pfeiffer

1 Lobby
2 Kitchen
3 Dining room
4 Living room
5 Terrace
6 Media room
7 Powder room
8 Bedroom
9 Dressing room
10 Bathroom

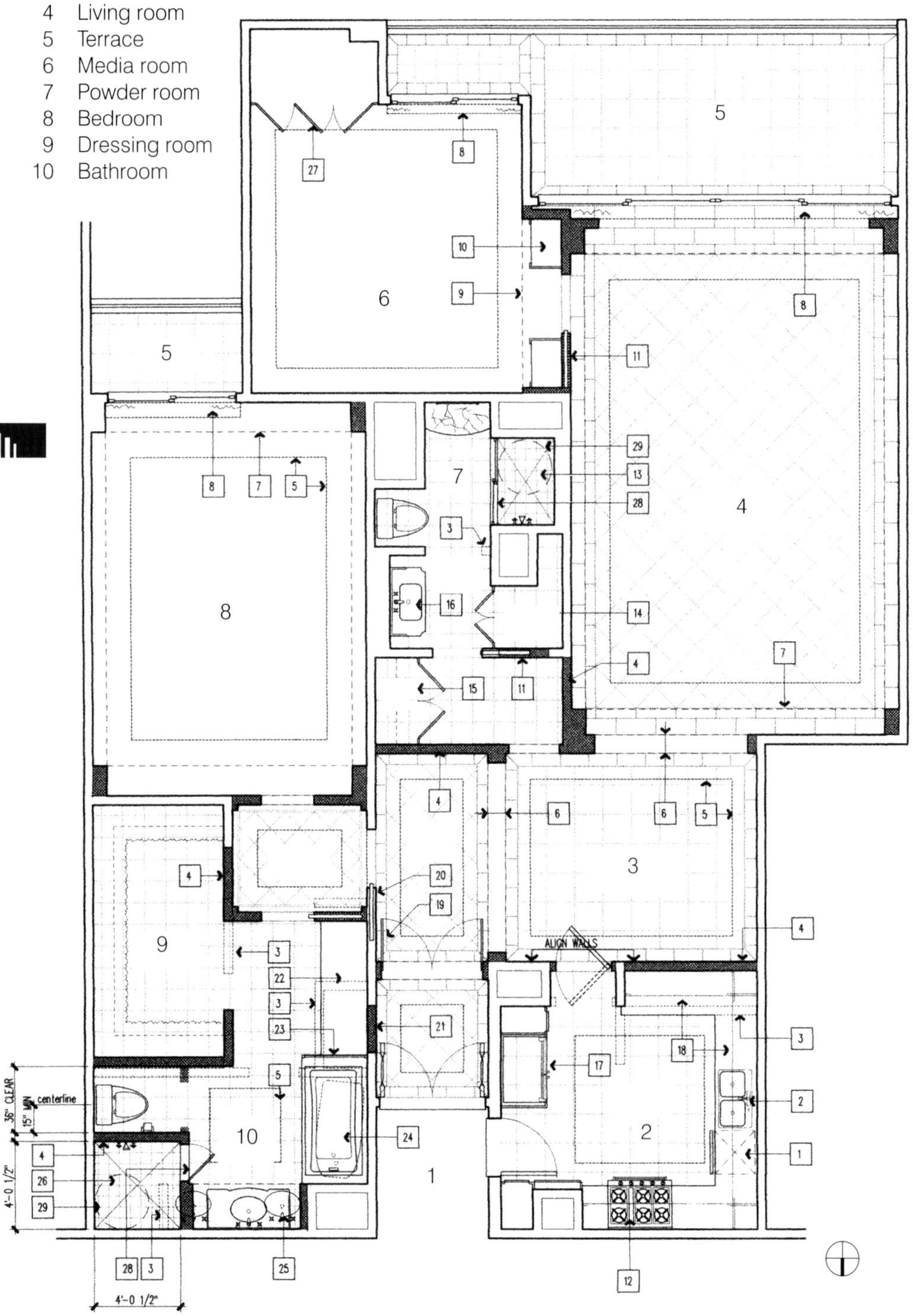

living large in london

London, United Kingdom

Form Design Architecture

The elliptical upper floor of this luxurious 2,900-square-foot duplex penthouse in London is a prominent local landmark, commanding spectacular panoramic city views to St Paul's Cathedral.

Carved out of the sixth and seventh floor shell spaces originally earmarked for two apartments by the developer, the spatial arrangement has been conceived around a route that draws the visitor through the apartment from the point of entry on the lower floor to the final revelation of the 360-degree view from the upper floor living space and covered alfresco dining area on the landscaped terrace.

A linear entry gallery terminates in an atrium area at the heart of the plan, which links the two floors of open-plan living space. A double-height wall plate rises through this volume, tracing the curved perimeter of the upper floor ellipse, and linking the disparate geometries of the two levels. The wall also provides a degree of enclosure, and acts as a backdrop for the central focus of the apartment: an elegant cantilevered oak and glass stair. Ascending the stair, the curve of the enclosing wall gently turns the visitor through 180 degrees to finally reveal the spectacular city view, focused on St Paul's to the south from the upper level living area and terrace.

On the lower floor, a bedroom wing is linked to the open-plan living/entertaining areas via a transitional space: a cosy, book-lined study located behind a sliding wall. When required, this can be closed to create a third bedroom—complete with bathroom discreetly concealed behind built-in joinery. The master suite and a further guest suite are also essentially open plan, but are fully divisible (when guests are staying) with a system of concealed, full-height doors.

The palette of materials is surprising but elegant: blue limestone, matt white lacquer joinery and paintwork, soft grey Venetian plaster for the curved plate wall, and steel and glass for the rest.

Initially nervous that the white finishes would result in an environment that was too clinical, the clients are now effusive about the tranquility and calm of their luminous, light-filled home, high above the traffic of London.

Photography: Matthew Weinreb

loft for a super hero

New York, New York, USA

Resolution: 4 Architecture

New York is home to some larger-than-life figures; some of them not quite human. In fact, some of them could easily be called 'super-human.' The editor-in-chief of Marvel Comics, Joe Quesada, should know. He's responsible for the fate (and hero status) of some of the city's most recognizable names, from the Hulk to Spiderman. He's not short on personality himself, so it's only fitting that he occupy an apartment that's rather grand.

The Loft for a Super Hero, which alludes more to Marvel's characters than Mr. Quesada, lest readers think he has an ego as big as Doctor Doom, is a thoroughly suitable space for a stable of personalities with impressive superpowers. Defined by oversized rooms and grand dimensions, the 4750-square-foot loft is located in a former industrial building in New York's Chelsea neighborhood, where it occupies an entire floor with full-window exposures and classic urban views. When Mr. Quesada and his family (small and extended) first moved in, the space had merit in terms of scale, but little intimacy. In short, it needed to be designed for more of a 'human' scale than a super hero one.

So a complete gut renovation was organized, with Resolution: 4 Architecture redesigning the loft to fit the needs of both the family and Mr. Quesada's work. Due to the depth of the extremely large floor plan, the space was demarcated into various zones with cabinets, which accommodated storage while allowing the 'loft-ness' of the space to flow through. The result is a spectacular space that works on all levels, and allows personal/private, family, and business to cohabit in a harmonious fashion.

The public zone consists of areas for the kitchen, dining, and living rooms, along with other areas for display, collections, and musical entertainment. These zones remain open, marked by furniture placement and lighting fixtures above. Natural light permeates the space and is diffused by the use of clear frosted glass and polycarbonate, creating a series of layered transparencies.

The private zone, which includes the master bedroom situated in the back of the space with a stunning view, directly on axis with the Empire State Building, is almost as eye-catching as the public areas. The master closet and bathroom are separated from the public zone by a 25-foot-long, floor-to-ceiling frosted glass pane. The guest bedroom, child's room, and playroom, meanwhile, are located on the front street side of the loft and are both united and separated by cabinets and frosted glass doors. In between these private zones are the semi-private home theater, the entry, the powder room, and the artist's studio.

To accommodate Mr. Quesada's large collection of comic artifacts, a large number of built-ins were devised to fit into the studio. The theater space is also designed in such a way that it allows the Quesadas to enjoy the flexibility of dissolving the theater in and out of the public space by simply opening or closing the large sliding glass doors.

With materials such as maple, teak, ceramic/glass tile, black steel, painted concrete, ebonized mahogany veneered plywood, stainless steel, frosted acrylic, and custom frosted glass, it is an exceptional mix of strong components and gentle spaces that both impresses and comforts all those who enter. Just as a superhero should do.

Photography: Floto Warner

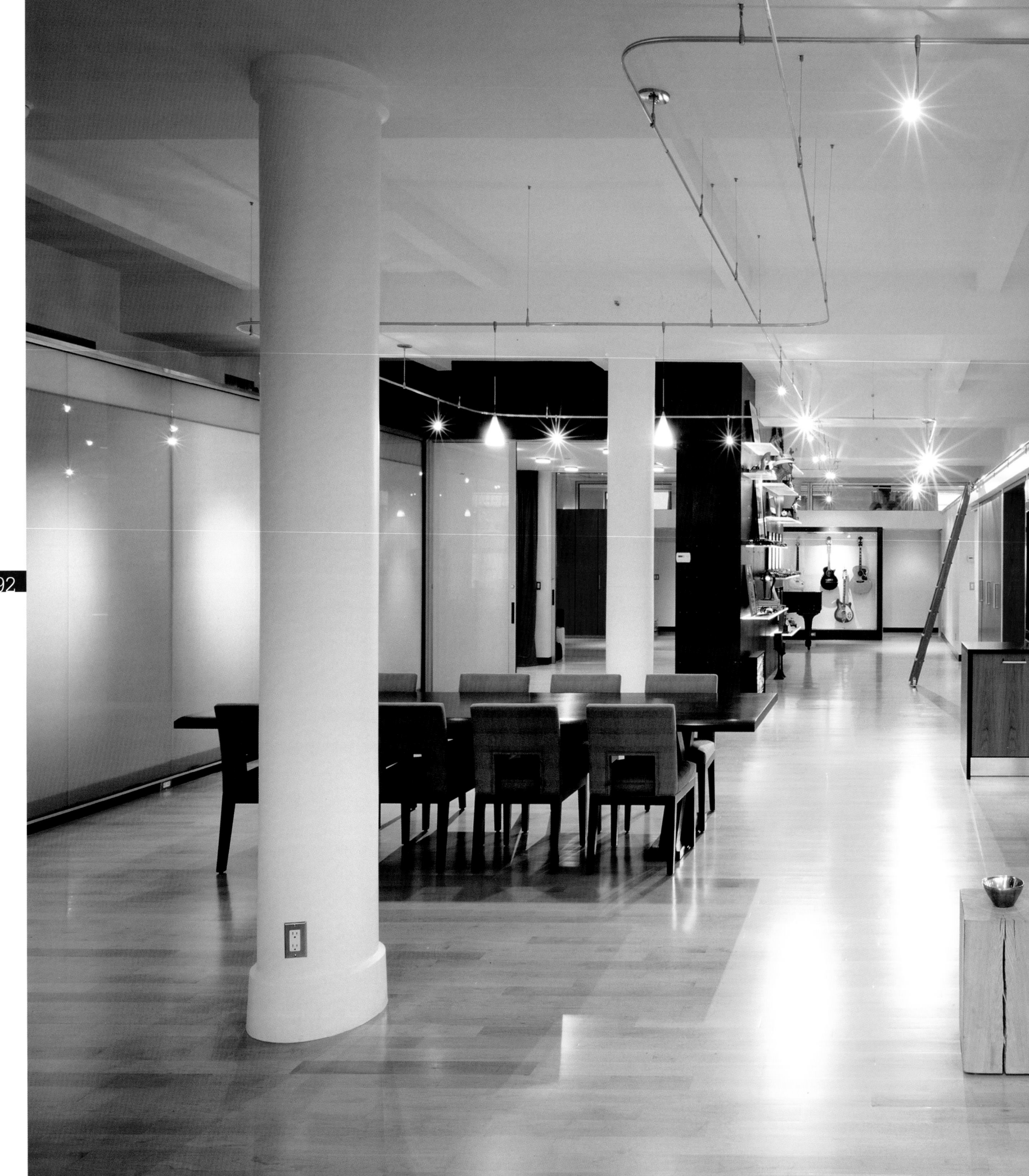

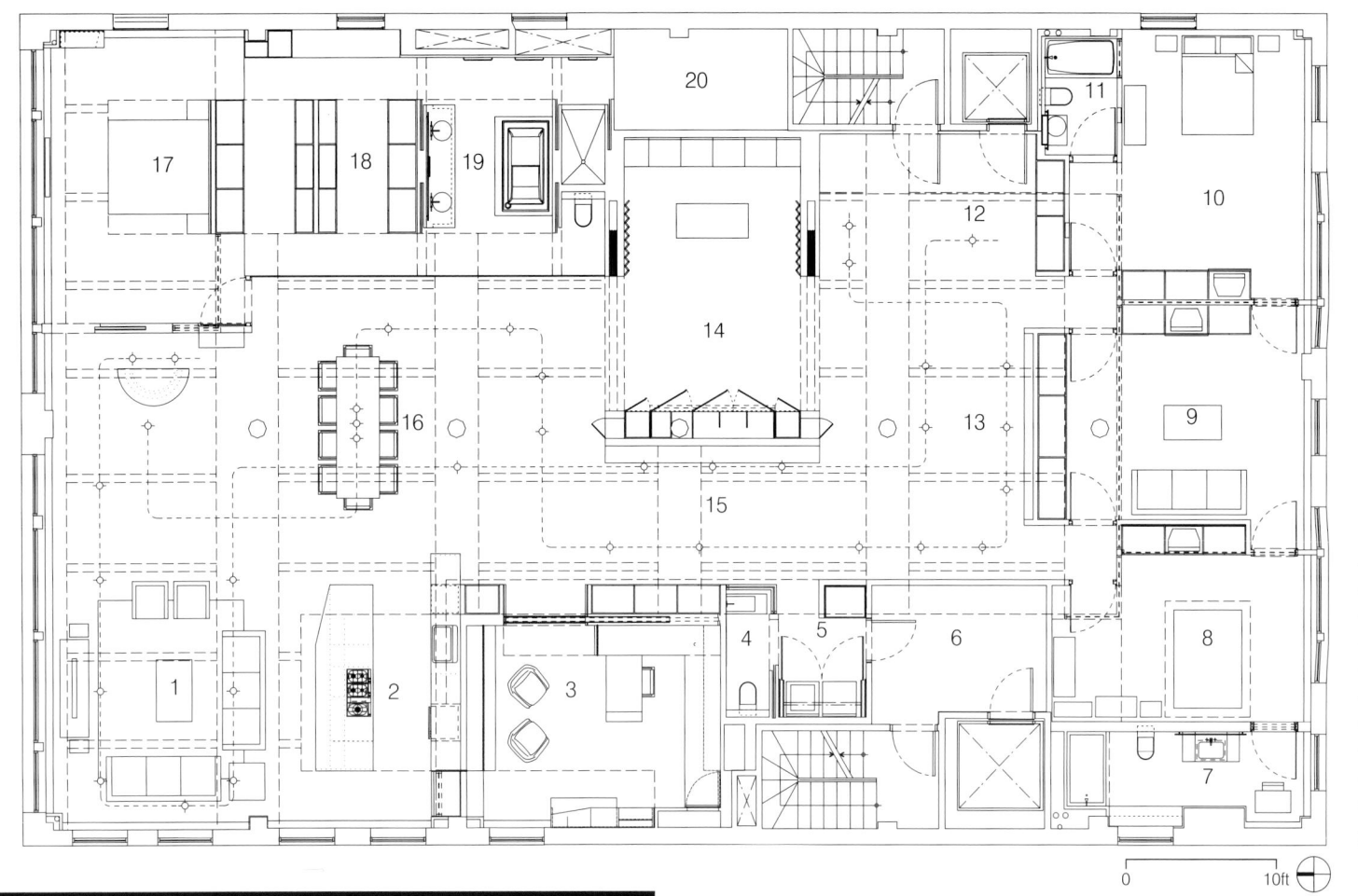

1   Living room
2   Kitchen
3   Studio
4   Powder room
5   Utility room
6   Storage
7   Bathroom
8   Bedroom
9   Playroom
10 Guest bedroom
11 Guest bathroom
12 Entry
13 Theater
14 Hall
15 Music area
16 Dining area
17 Master bedroom
18 Master closet
19 Master bathroom
20 Storage

0   10ft

manhattan transfer

New York, New York, USA

Smith-Miller + Hawkinson Architects

New York architects designing spectacular spaces with fantastic views in Manhattan often face a problem: whether to embellish the interior, or whether to leave it unadorned and simple so it doesn't compete with the vistas? When it came to designing the interior for this TriBeCa penthouse, Henry Smith-Miller went for the latter option. The view was so amazing, he reasoned, it would be a crime to simply dismiss it and block it out with a 'busy' interior. Instead Smith-Miller designed an apartment that is almost like a stage: elegant, and filled with only a few evocative pieces of furniture. The strategy worked, because the penthouse is now a dramatic, ongoing, multi-act play where the interior forms the stage and the twinkling city outside form the storyline.

In order to create this grand space, Smith-Miller remodeled the former multi-bedroom abode into an open-plan loft-style dwelling. This strategy had two aims: to 'open' up the space and make it bigger and more inviting, and—more importantly—to create more visual connections to the northern and southern exposures. Before the renovation, the apartment consisted of an upper level with two bathrooms and a dim, two-bedroom dormitory-style space, and a lower level with the main living rooms. After the renovation, the apartment is now an airy, light-filled home with views that make its owner glad to be in Manhattan. One bathroom on the second level was relocated in order to create a large music room on the mezzanine with northern views, while the master bedroom was transformed into an enormous suite with a deep, soaking tub that extends out over the living space below and offers views of the city skyline outside. The new stairs also offer views of Manhattan from the mid-level landing, while a clear glass balustrade provides clear views from the apartment through the stairs to the city beyond.

On the lower floor, the new configuration of spaces has seen a glamorous entertaining area open up that is perfect for parties, with a living room highlighted by a fireplace, a library/study, an open dining area, a galley kitchen, and a media room. The rich palette of materials chosen adds further gloss to the already distinguished space, and includes Swiss pear wood, pale limestone tiles, and subtle steel and glass. Custom-made bamboo treads on the staircase match the flooring at each level and provide a continuous flow between the upper and lower floors.

It is an apartment that is quietly perfect: full of space to breathe, move, and party, and yet intimate enough and high above the city to feel as though you're right away from it all.

Photography: Matteo Piazza

miami glamor

Miami, Florida, USA
Archiforma

Miami architecture has always been in the international spotlight. In a design world dominated by monochromatic palettes, minimalist angles, and too-cool-for-school designers, Miami's surprisingly flamboyant, startlingly colored, and wildly daring offerings stand out like the unexpectedly talented but slightly boho wild child in a class of earnest, black-clad students. While every other hotelier and architect tries to be hip—and occasionally succeeds—Miami is hip, without even trying.

Standing tall among the sweeping curves and lavish ornamentation of this architectural fantasy land is a new project that is making people sit up and talk. In fact, The Setai has been gathering media attention ever since it opened. The hipster's travel guide, *Mr and Mrs Smith*, described it having a "Zen-like tranquility," and there is no doubt its quiet lines sit in contrast to the rest of Miami's over-the-top, 'look-at-me' architecture. This is not to say it's all sombre understatement. There are certainly ample amounts of luxury touches and Miami-esque fantasy elements to remind you that you are indeed in the home of the big, the brave, and the brash. But it does raise the standard for Florida-style living.

The Setai is actually divided into two parts: a five-star resort hotel in one and a 40-story tower of high-luxe residential apartments in the other. Residents in the latter can enjoy the services of the former, making them feel as though they're permanently on holiday and/or living the life of a famous rock star on a lavish tour. Mick Jagger would certainly feel right at home in one of these apartments—Suite 3106, which is a truly extravagant home in the clouds that's one part glamor and nine parts pure decadence.

Designed to complement the bright open space of the South Beach area outside, the Archiforma-designed interior of this fantastic space offers great walls of glass that grab the view while simultaneously blocking it out at the touch of a button via high-tech blinds.

Described by Archiforma as a 'pure fantasy,' the penthouse stands apart for its customized fit-out. The apartment features polished white granite slabs on the spacious balcony, hand-dyed leather tiles on the wall, wenge wood doors, wallpaper made from suede, and bathrooms crafted from Biana Carrera marble. Glossy wall and floor finishes capture the light—an integral part of Miami life—while enormous windows frame the view.

As with many modern apartment buildings, there is a great deal of flow between inside and outside, and not just via the windows. In fact the design at the Setai positively encourages people to get out and make the most of the luxury playground, both inside the grounds and out in Miami itself. The gardens around the tower include a series of magnificent pools, each heated to a different temperature, so guests and residents can choose from 70-, 80- or 90-degree water, before perhaps going for a plunge into the refreshingly cold ocean outside. Residents are also permitted to make the most of the 24-hour room service and round-the-clock concierge offered in the hotel section, which includes maid service and massages.

Such is the success of Suite 3106 that Majestic Properties has put it on the market—for a cool $3.25 million. Rock stars take note.

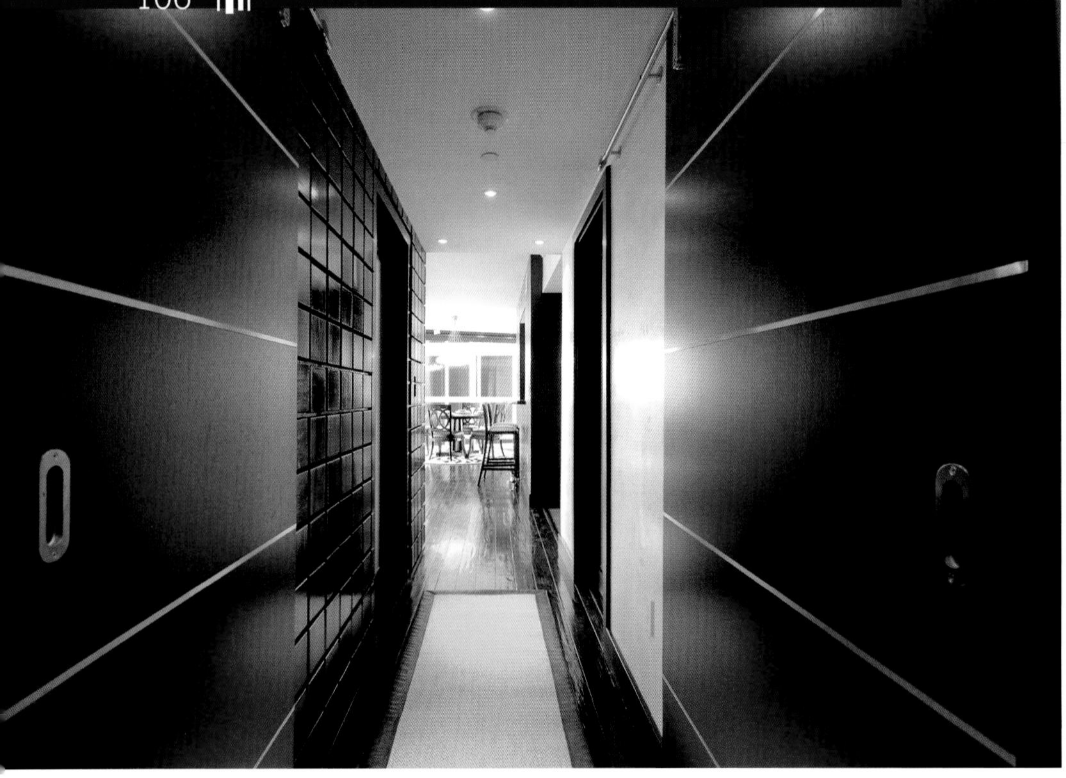

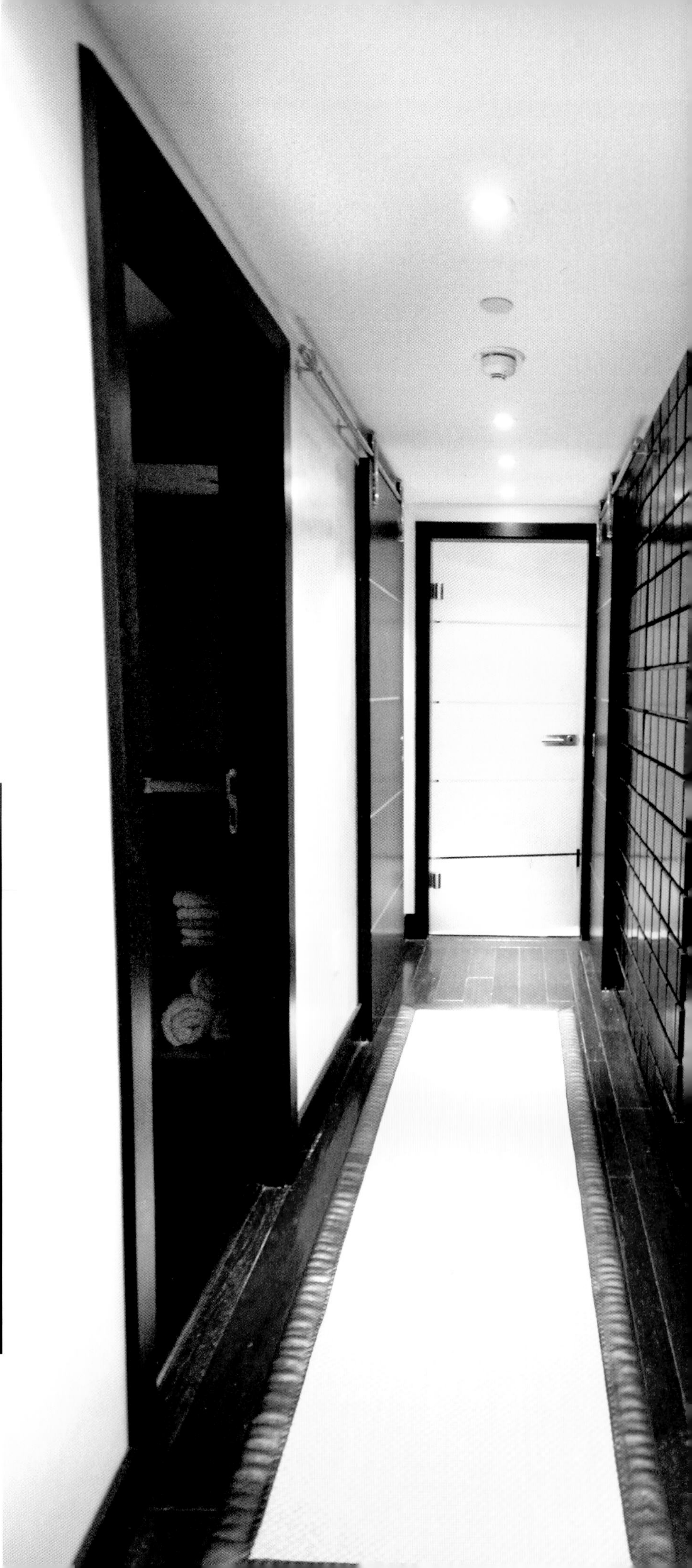

new york,
new york

New York, New York, USA

Louise Braverman,
Architect

Many of us are familiar with the New York style of apartment, having seen hundreds of them in the movies and on television, from *Six Degrees of Separation* to *You've Got Mail*, *Sex and the City*, and *Alfie*. We know the spaces can be compact and the architecture no-nonsense (in that very New York way). And we know that despite these things, living in Manhattan amidst the skyscrapers and high-density life is one of the most invigorating things one can do.

This is partly because of the views. New York apartments, if they're positioned in the right spot, offer some of the most intoxicating views an urbanite could ask for. The very lucky (and very rich) have views of the Empire State Building, the rivers, and places like Central Park; the rest remain content with the vistas of close-knit life in their vertical villages. A view opens up the space, and gives perspective of the city. It reminds New Yorkers of their fortune, and also drives them on to more ambitious things. Like a better view, for example.

This apartment is the epitome of New York-style living. Set high in a tower overlooking Central Park, it features luxuriously long spaces, groovy furniture and—best of all—views to shake a martini to. When architect Louise Braverman was first commissioned to overhaul it though, it wasn't nearly as spectacular. And the extraordinary views, which included sightlines to Central Park, certainly weren't being used to their full potential. So she set about maximizing not only the variability of the space but also the vistas, creating a place that fused sight lines on the outside with quiet lines in the inside. "The main goal of the project was to open it up and bring in the light," she says. She gutted most of the interior and positioned new walls to achieve uninterrupted sightlines. "I wanted to create axial and cross-axial views to get the sense you are in a tower."

The strategy worked. The spatial manipulation succeeded in making the apartment seem bigger, while sliding doors provided further flexibility, reconfiguring spaces depending on the need.

The color palette is predominantly white, which is soothing on the eye after the flurry of urban grays and blacks experienced on the street below. To brighten what could be a glacial interior, Braverman introduced flashes of Hermès-inspired orange, which add a theatrical traffic light-style touch. In the living room, the tan chairs almost reflect the windows of the apartment towers outside, which stretch on into the navy blue distance. In the living room, a hide-covered ottoman and an abstract work of art with orange as its primary tone mirror the cubist shapes of the skyscrapers outside, while the rest of the neo-retro pieces, including a 1950's 'womb chair', add life and form.

Finally, the bedroom is a glamorous mix of white and silver, which also reflect the color palette of Manhattan. Thanks to these cool shades, and the abundance of light, the apartment has an ethereal quality—which is fitting considering it's high in the clouds. It's also an elegant space to relax and stare out at Central Park, now framed eloquently by sophisticated windows, and to watch the changing plays of shades as the famous park dances through the seasons.

1   Entry
2   Living
3   Bedroom
4&5 Bathroom
6   Bedroom
7   Dining room
8   Bathroom
9   Kitchen

0   10ft

paris match

Paris, France
Alex Mony

As apartments and architecture go, there is nothing quite like the inimitable, eternally elegant Palais Royal for sheer glamour. Hidden away in a forgotten little enclave of Paris, within a whisper of the Louvre but strangely set aside from the bustle of the city, it is a square of extraordinary architecture and charm. To reach it, residents and visitors have to pass through a tiny arcade, then through an inner courtyard, until finally they reach the magnificent rectangle, bordered on three sides by extraordinary Victor Louis-designed buildings and a sublimely designed garden. Wandering through its arches and down its arcade is a step into another time. And even more so at night when the watchmen close the garden, leaving the moonlit square to the enjoyment of the fortunate few who reside here.

Set on the edge of this architecturally beautiful square, this luxurious duplex defines what it is to live in the City of Light. Inside, there is light, style, and classic French elegance. Outside, there is more of the same, with the fiercely disciplined lines of the famous Parisian garden forming a perfect, poetic vista to look out upon. It is a true example of an apartment matching the interior and the architecture to the surrounds and to the view: a perfect match of line and style.

The 140-square-meter apartment is set on the fourth and fifth floors of one of the famous Victor Louis-designed wings of this elegant rectangle. The spacious floor plan extends outside, thanks to a grand balcony with views directly over the historic gardens, and a glamorous terrace with table and chairs overlooking rue Montpensier. Both of these exterior living spaces give the apartment depth, while offering eye-catching spaces to entertain, or simply sit and reflect with a newspaper and coffee as the morning sun wakes up the square.

The ground floor of the apartment consists of the principal living spaces—the living room, the dining room, the kitchen, the balcony, a bedroom, a bathroom, and an ensuite. On the next level, there are two more bedrooms, two full bathrooms, and the terrace. The two floors are accessed by a staircase, which winds its way up from the living room to the next level.

When the owner took possession of the apartment, it had potential as a living space, but he wanted it to be flexible enough to rent out to tourists. He knew the elegant Parisian architecture, including the molded ceilings, the parquetry floors, the elegant fireplace, and the floor-to-ceiling French windows that open onto the balcony would appeal, but he also understood that it had to offer an 'international' style of interior design, which meant that it had to be mostly French in feel but still have all the modern comforts that appeal to global travelers. So he ensured each bedroom had its own ensuite, with enclosed bathtubs and American showers. He also installed a large walk-in closet and grand ensuite bathroom next to the bedroom on the lower floor. Then he furnished it with modern accoutrements, such as a juice maker, coffee maker, and four televisions, all without losing the Parisian charm of the design.

Now, the renovated duplex is a highly luxurious home away from home for all those who are fortunate enough to pass through, whether the owner, his friends, or simply those visitors privileged enough to enjoy a prolonged stay.

paris perfect

Paris, France
Alex Mony

Paris apartments tend to fall into two decorating camps. There are those that are full of the collections of their Parisian owners, and are therefore cluttered with much-loved *objets trouvés*. And there are those that are pared-back, tightly glamorous spaces, where clean lines and elegance rule. This stylish apartment falls into the latter category: it is as beautifully designed as the famous Palais Royal square it sits on.

Decorated in smart French blue, with walls etched in a crisp white trim, it has many of the elements found in sophisticated Parisian abodes: a grand salon, herringbone parquetry flooring, molded ceilings, dignified marble fireplaces, grand drapes, and beautifully designed cabinetry. But it also contains quirky touches and whimsical vignettes that are a reflection of the personality of the owner, from a classic, old-fashioned typewriter in the living room to bold apple green walls in the kitchen and bedroom. Recently renovated, in such a way that the original charm of the place has been retained, the 100-square-meter space has been transformed from a beautiful but slightly faded and definitely dated interior to a polished and thoroughly modern one. The changes were subtle— a splash of French blue paint, wireless broadband technology, a new coffee maker in the kitchen—things that its owner describes as making the apartment full of "modern comforts, but in a traditional French style." But together, the updates give this grand old dame a whole new lease of life.

Perhaps the most spectacular thing about this Parisian abode is its vista. Located directly atop the symmetrical magnificence of the historic Palais Royal, in the third floor of an graceful old 17th-century building, it commands a view of the garden and forecourt that makes guests stop in their tracks. The apartment's enormous windows make a feature of this view, while the pale green walls pick up the colors of the famous clipped trees and lawns.

Now a quietly luxurious space to retreat to in this very chic corner of the city, the two-bedroom apartment is one part refined style, one part sublime views, and two parts sheer comfort.

pure
positano

Positano, Italy

lazzarini pickering architetti

The word 'Positano' immediately conjures up a hedonistic level of luxe: Camparis at luncheon, Frangelicos at night, and all manner of decadence in between. Add to this mix a villa designed by architect Carl Pickering of lazzarini pickering architetti and you have all the ingredients for a splendid time.

Interestingly, it was the coastline of Italy, and the easy lifestyle it inspires, that served as a significant influence on Pickering during the design of the deluxe hideaway. The architect envisaged a space far away from it all: an airy escape from the noise and bustle of Italy's famous cities. Ironically, the house in which the apartment is situated originally formed part of an 18th-century villa that belonged to a monastery, so the provenance was right for a place of peace and contemplation.

The original floor plan comprised a kitchen, dining, two guest bedrooms and bathrooms on the ground floor, a living area and master bedroom on the first floor, and a principal living and entertainment space in between, connecting both. There was a view, too, a great sweeping perspective of blue that epitomized Italy's coastline in a perfect vignette. But sadly, none of these elements were being used to their full potential, so Pickering set about designing a space that was more in keeping with a contemporary retreat on the cliffs of Positano's famously chic coastline. Keeping in mind the architectural traditions of the area, and the importance of setting such a place ever so carefully against the historical context of the ancient seaside town (the Amalfi Coast was once held under Arab control, which led to the region's love of ceramic tiles and Moorish architecture) he came up with four architectural elements that transformed the villa while linking it to its traditional past. The first was a wide staircase that joined the mid-level living area and the first floor one. A striking architectural statement in itself, it did more than just provide a walkway between floors: it provided a space to play and display. Next, he designed a 'flying sofa'

sitting area of 3.2 by 3 meters that was cantilevered at a height of 2 meters into the 6-meter-high portico, serving as a spectacular entertainment space. He also introduced a 6-meter by 2.4-meter sleeping platform that included a bathing area. Lastly, he linked the lot with a visual 'ribbon' of color that joined the portico living and kitchen spaces. This tile ribbon, which was dressed in 18th- and 19th-century tiles, begins at the ceiling, descends the 6-meter-high space, forms a bench upon which to work or pour drinks for guests, enters the floor, folds down to become the dining table and then folds back up to the ceiling where it bends and eventually disappears.

On top of these elements, Pickering placed an abundance of cushions and bolsters, made to the architect's design by the producers of Fendi Casa. To continue the heady color scheme, the bed base and bedspread were covered in lime green and hot pink striped linens sourced from Manuel Canovas. The vibrant tones perfectly suit the setting, with its wide blue sky and shimmering ocean, and also the villa's pool. Finally, to finish the modern, living-on-the-edge feel, Pickering selected a scattering of fabulously edgy furniture, from a sofa by Edra to a gathering of 'Tulip' chairs by Saarinen.

Together, the space and the pieces within it serve to create an extraordinary home: a truly modern escape that nods its hat to the past while looking cheekily ahead to the future.

roman holiday

Rome, Italy
Studio Transit

Studio Transit, based in southern Italy, is well-known for its interior design and town planning. The latter role has taught Studio Transit's architects how to balance the needs of modern clients with the preservation of Italy's celebrated artistic and architectural legacy.

This apartment, situated in a grand, whitewashed, 17th-century palazzo high above the roofline of Rome, posed many of the usual challenges in buildings such as this. Past and present had to be married together without affecting or upsetting one or the other. Furthermore, the steeply pitched ceilings and exposed wooden beams couldn't be destroyed, although they were certainly in need of repair and modernization. In short, just the right touch of modernity needed to be grafted onto the apartment's very old bones, without denting the ambiance in the process.

Studio Transit started with the view. Undoubtedly the residence's best feature, this vista is breathtaking. The top of the 17th-century palazzo looks out over a maze of narrow streets circling the Pantheon, and past that to the glorious baroque church spires of the city. Studio Transit's main priority was to marry this interior with the city views outside, while still retaining a sense of privacy within the dwelling. The firm also had to find a way of combining contemporary components, such as stainless steel and glass, with both the historical heritage of the city outside and the owners' antique furnishings, which included family heirlooms dating back to the 18th century.

Studio Transit's architects did this by keeping the interior free from architectural clutter. The sloping ceilings were retained, as were the wooden beams, but asymmetrical openings were carved out of the original walls to create new and contemporary living spaces. These were done in such a way that the principal living spaces were set within an open-plan interior but were still clearly defined. This had the added benefit of creating a loft-style atmosphere—which gave the place a funky look right from the start. The floors were left clear, while furniture was carefully selected for its minimalist lines so as not to disturb the serenity of the space. The white upholstered sofas and stool were also given wheels, to allow them mobility and flexibility.

To link the main living area with the terrace, a freestanding and beautifully sculptural spiral staircase was fashioned from aluminum panels, while windows were left unadorned to allow the view to be framed all day long. With its twisted, helicoid shape, the staircase mirrored the baroque towers captured in this view, creating a subtle play of pattern and line between inside and out.

In the kitchen, sleek, stainless steel cabinets brought the space into the 21st century, while offering a surprisingly sensitive backdrop for the English oak table and chairs. A similar strategy was devised for the dining room, where edgy Cassina chairs add a hip touch to the 19th-century dining table.

New but still old, and funky but still classic, the apartment is now a cool, timeless place to retreat to from the hustle and bustle of modern Rome.

Photography: Giovanna Piemont

a sense of place

Paris, France
Alex Mony

The oldest square in Paris, Place des Vosges, originally named Place Royale, is the prototype for the urban square. A proper geometric square (140 meters by 140 meters), it has inspired other grand city rectangles, such as New York's Union Square and London's famous Bloomsbury Square. Yet when it was first built, the now-impressive place and its 36 elegant townhouses were a radical shift in urban planning. Previously, Parisians had been accustomed to living in separate hotels. With the Place des Voges, they were now residing beside each other, and sharing the same garden. But the trend caught on quickly, thanks to one of the Place des Voges' homeowners, Henri IV and his queen, who both maintained houses on the square (identified by the higher roofs at the north and south entrances), although they never lived in them. Another distinguishing aspect of the square is that all the façades were built to the same design: elegant red brick ornamented with stone detailing and steeply pitched blue slate roofs, all set over vaulted arcades. For many years, it was the place to see, and be seen, and still remains an elegant address even today.

Looking out over this symmetry and greenery is an apartment that reflects the calm of the famous square. Renovated by Alex Mony, it still features the angled wooden beams and architectural charm that is typical of many Parisian apartments, but has been modernized to offer a sympathetic mix of old and new. The principal living area, distinguished by its angular roofline and dormer-style windows, is a delightful open-plan space that doesn't once feel cloistered, as some Parisian apartments do, perhaps due to the white paintwork, which 'lightens' the space while allowing the beams to show through. Floorboards also keep the apartment 'clean' of visual clutter.

The light-filled living room isn't grand, although it does have a magnificent fireplace, but it feels as though it's on top of the world, thanks to the beautiful windows, which frame the view. Mony has also deliberately edited the furniture down to a few key pieces, a strategy that keeps the space elegant. The daybed is a quintessential French design, while the table and chairs are quirky but stylish—again, very French.

In the bedrooms, the same elegantly sloping walls remind you that you're in Paris, while a swirl of script on the wall in one of the rooms adds a playful touch.

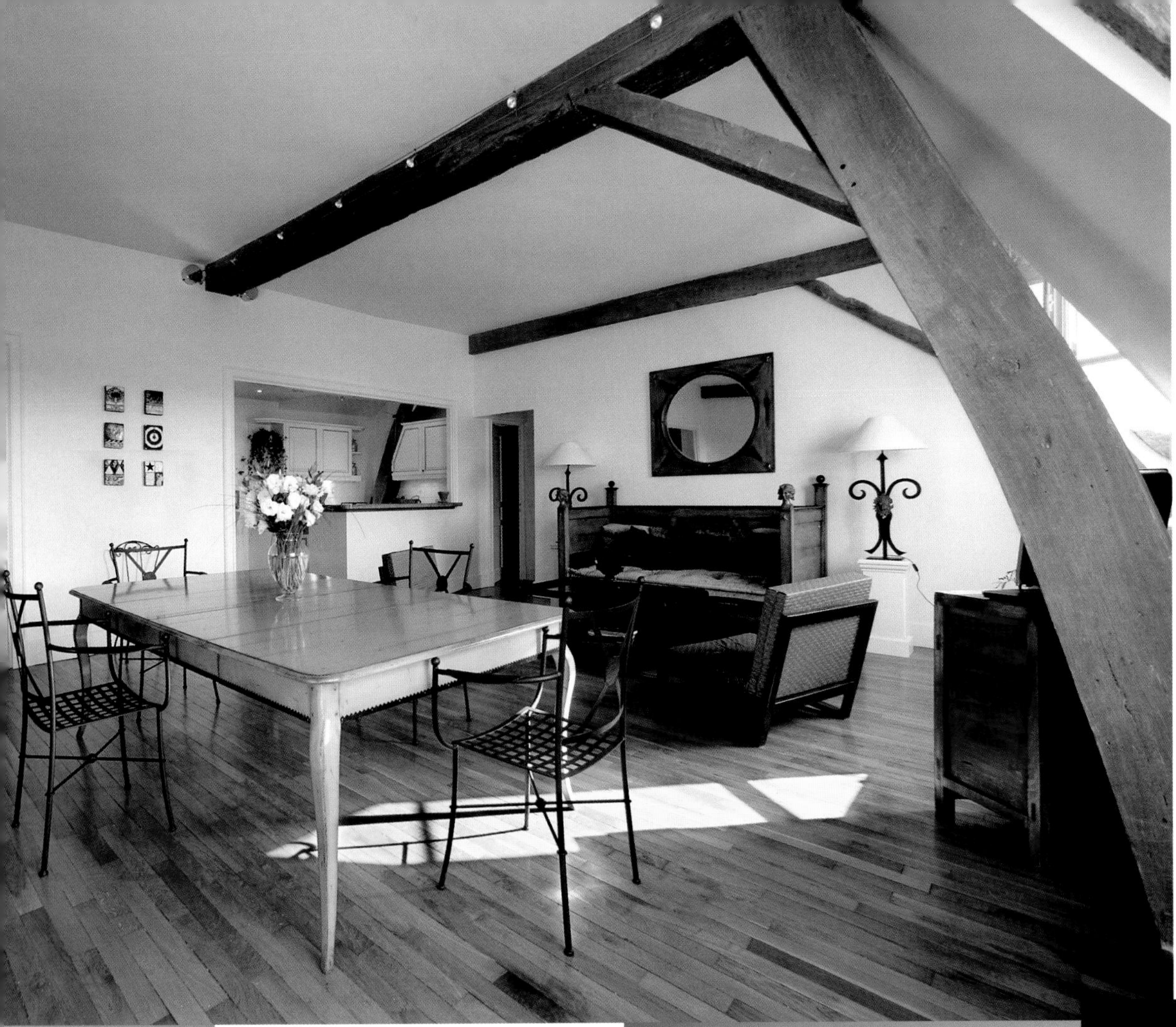

« Là tout n'est qu'ordre et beauté,
Luxe, calme et volupté »

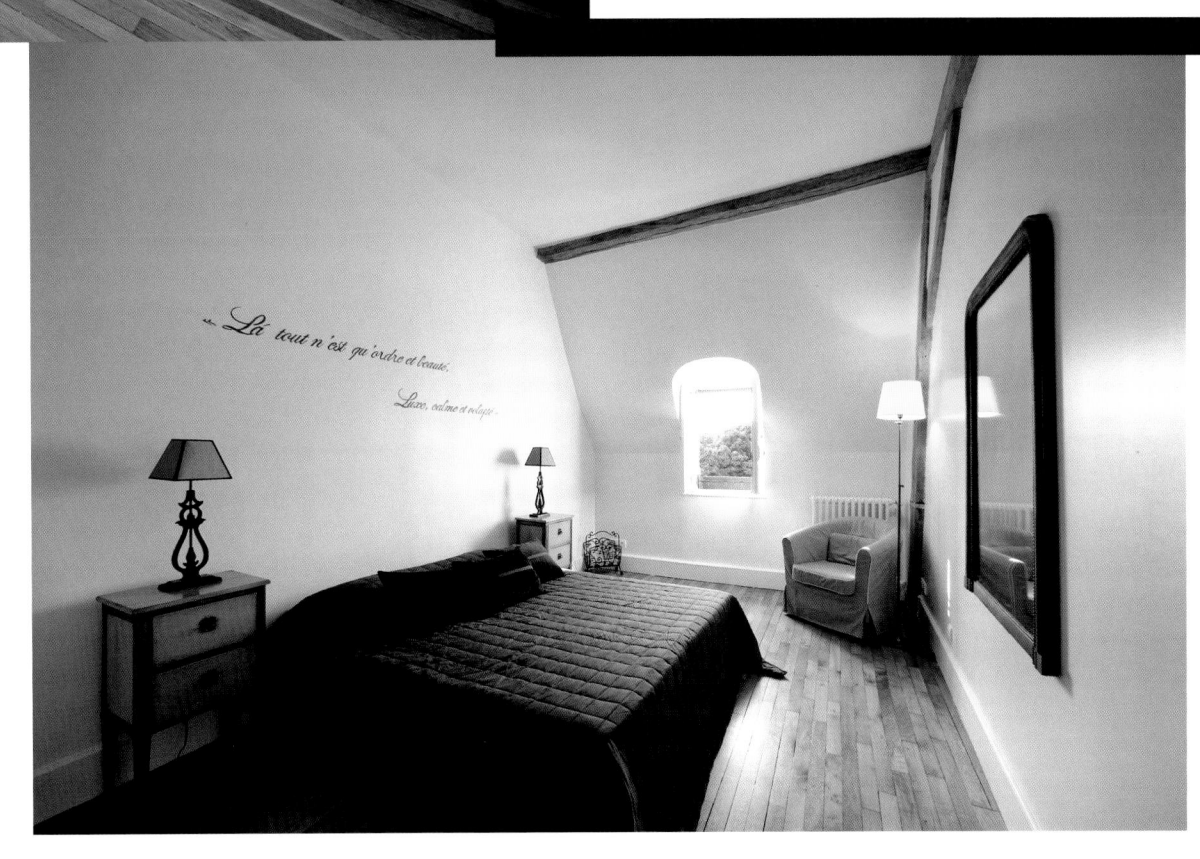

simple luxuries

Monaco, Monte Carlo

Claudio Silvestrin

Claudio Silvestrin's work needs no introduction to architecture aficionados. The master of minimalism has established a global reputation for creating spare but extraordinarily beautiful spaces that have little in them but lots of detail. A celebration of the purity of form and the clarity of mind, they are some of the most sublime buildings ever designed in the modern age. Austere but not extreme, elegant but not ostentatious, and contemporary yet timeless.

This clifftop penthouse in Monaco is a perfect example. Pure Silvestrin, it is a serene place of calm, reflection, and respite, along with heart-stopping views. Built in the 1970s and converted to a modern residence in 2006, the two-story apartment has a south-facing vista that includes a spectacularly panoramic view of the sea on the Côte d'Azur. To make the most of this vista, Silvestrin opened up the living room, and also cleared it of clutter, so the emphasis was solely on the view. The north–south axes were also cleared of impediments to make room for a perspective that links the master bedroom and bathroom with the living room, thus creating a visual flow that unites day living with night life. As well, the first and second floors are linked by a majestic limestone cylindrical wall, which embraces the spiral stairs that lead to the upper kitchen and spacious roof terrace. These strong shapes and rigorous geometry—all very Silvestrin—add a sense of solemnity but also an exquisite, monastic-style elegance. Some may dismiss them as overly minimalist, and there is no doubt Silvestrin's work has advanced the popularity of minimalism— but there is also a quiet sophistication to the space. Without the clutter of modern life or the frivolous accoutrements of contemporary living, the apartment seems cleaner, streamlined, and also more pleasing to be in than a normal penthouse filled with luxury fillings. Even the furniture and fittings, including the six-meter-long island bar, with its bronze sheet top, and the limestone bathtub that resembles a shell, have been designed by Silvestrin to be understated. So understated, in fact, they almost disappear into the architecture.

Immaculate, and untainted by the clutter and flotsam and jetsam of modern life, it is a cool, calm, and composed abode: a serene tribute to pared-back design at its very best. As Sir Terence Conran said of his contemporary, "Silvestrin is a sculptor of space, and a great artist in the same way that Mondrian, Rothko, Arp, and Caro are … His work is simply sublime."

sydney vista

Sydney, New South Wales, Australia
Abode

The trouble with designing an apartment that looks out over Sydney's spectacular harbor is that it takes a lot to come up with something that will meet the high aesthetic standards demanded of the extraordinary site. The city's finest feature is so sublime in its natural beauty, architects and designers have to continually think of new ways to compete with it, and draw the eye inwards, to their interiors, rather than out, to the cool view of blue. This is not to say that architects and designers bemoan the task of designing for harborside locales. On the contrary, many relish the challenge of renovating or reworking residences fronting the water. The trick is to create a seamless merger of vista and interior, so that one doesn't overpower the other, and that both sit happily in each other's eye-catching presence.

Rod Smith of Abode knows the difficulty of designing such a place. When he was commissioned to take on a low-rise apartment at Darling Point in Sydney's inner east, with views of the famous bridge, he knew it would be a challenge to compete with the scene. The added difficulty was that the apartment is set down low, and so the view, while still spectacular, is 'flatter' than those residences at the top of high-rises. *Vogue Living* magazine described the site as being "divided evenly into five horizontal bands: terrace, pool, park, harbor and city skyline," and it's easy to see where the problems could lie in such a juxtaposition of visuals. Make the furniture too high and the pieces are immediately out of proportion. Make the pool too square, and it's instantly out of sync with the elongated nature of the other elements. Make the colors too brassy, and they're simply not right for the palette of Sydney-esque hues, which include cool blues and yacht-sail whites.

Half the solution had already been found, in the form of a bank of folding, aluminum-framed doors. Spanning the full width of the apartment, when open, thus create an unrestricted indoor/outdoor living area, complete with black-tiled plunge pool, that merges the glamorous view and entertainment area with the privacy required for inside. The interior space works because it is deep, and the furniture is kept deliberately low-slung, to continue the horizontal feel. The key pieces—including a couple of sexy sofas and some white Mies van der Rohe Barcelona chairs—are comfortable and chic but don't interrupt the sight lines, particularly those of the city skylines.

In addition, the color palette is quiet and calm. Deep mushrooms, gentle smoky grays, and rich thoroughbred and chocolate browns provide a luxurious gallery space for the owners' collection of Asian and African artifacts and antiques, with down lighting highlighting the artwork areas. The natural and artificial lighting also enables the mood of the apartment to change, from charmingly bright during the day to intimate and serene at night. It's a handsome space: dignified, refined, quiet. And it neither outdoes or is intimidated by the view. Both sit happily side by side, perhaps because both are on the same level. Ironically, one of the owners lived in an apartment on the upper floor for several years before deciding to move down here—"it was closer to the view," he claimed, adding that it had a "better sense of space and flow." Rod Smith has done much with a difficult location, creating a place to stay, play, swim, drink, and stare out at all that blue without feeling either cramped in the downstairs space, or too much on show. A site for sore eyes has become a setting of pleasure.

Photography: Georgina Moxham

terrace for two

New York, New York, USA
aardvarchitecture

A view of New York's Central Park and its urban woodlands, lawns, lakes, and refreshing greenery amid the grey heart of Manhattan is rare enough, but when that view makes up your entire living room window, you know you've found somewhere very special indeed. This penthouse, situated on the northwestern edge of Central Park, is surrounded by extraordinary uninterrupted views to the south, west and north; many of which capture the verdant splendor of New York's most famous park. The apartment is set so high on the city's skyline that you don't notice the noise, the traffic, and the madness. All you can see is a serene blanket of green. It is its own micro-oasis in the heart of the buzzing metropolis.

The apartment's original organization of rooms was based on a typical 1920s pinwheel structure. Efficient and intelligent, this floor plan showed great potential, including the promise of offering an aesthetically pleasing spatial continuity right through the apartment these oblique view lines. On the down side, the façade openings and existing windows did little to extend those suggested view lines out towards the surrounding skyline.

Despite the apparent challenges, the architecture firm responsible for the penthouse's transition from dated to daring was undaunted. Christian Volkmann and Lynette Widder of aardvarchitecture knew that the apartment's best assets were these priceless vistas. After all, when you are privy to such perspectives, it's only natural to want to frame them as a form of living art. So they set about prioritizing them in the program. However, in doing so they came across an unexpected dilemma: how to create a seamless flow and balance between the smaller details of the interior and the grander details—and scale—of the deep, urban views?

The solution? An apartment in which the views weren't shut off and framed like a painting behind glass but connected to the living space by the use of indoor/outdoor areas, including a stylish wraparound terrace. In this way, the apartment residents could 'connect' to the city and its myriad vistas, and form a relationship with Manhattan that was more meaningful than just a mansion in the sky. The relationship between interior and perspective became an almost intimate one. This was achieved by reconfiguring the spaces so that they embraced the view, and also flowed out to the terrace, leading people from inside to out, from glassed-in view to full-blown real-life skyline.

The master bathroom, for example, was originally separated from the west-facing terrace by a closet. By removing this closet, cutting a new opening into the brick cavity wall façade, and then positioning the bathtub immediately next to the new window, the experience of bathing was made far more dramatic. More importantly, the dialogue, and thus the relationship, between interior and skyline was strengthened. The bathroom was a mammoth task in itself, as the solid stone slab bathtub and shower basin, which was prefabricated in Germany, had to be shipped to the US in jigsaw puzzle-like pieces, and slowly installed over the course of two days. The coordination of things like plumbing and dimensional tolerances, all the responsibility of the architect, was an immense challenge.

The relationship between interior and exterior was further articulated by the redesign of the terrace, undoubtedly the apartment's next best feature. By changing the heights of the window sills and enlarging the openings, a datum was created that links both sides of the wall and connects the two environments.

Photography: Paul Rivera archphoto

Planters for the garden were integrated into built-ins (in the form of cubic stainless steel containers), and encouraged the line of sight from terrace greenery to Central Park splendor. A series of wooden boxes surrounding these planters conceal an irrigation system, outdoor speakers, air-conditioning exhaust outlets, and strip lighting, which creates a continuous glow at the base of the terrace wall at night and provides adequate exterior lighting without competing with the lights of the skyline. A stainless steel cable trellis system on the south and west terrace walls extends the layer of plant life upwards, so that the built-ins and the garden they house are read as a continuous threshold between apartment and terrace.

In the living room, meanwhile, the color palette has been reduced down to a simple, but elegant white, which is not only calming in the gunmetal grey mania of Manhattan but puts the focus firmly back on the view of Central Park and its seasonal changes, from vibrant green in summer to gold in fall and handsome black in the middle of winter. No matter what the season, the mood or light of the skyline, or even the weather, the apartment captures New York's beauty in all its grandeur and glamor from a design that is subtle, but remarkable. In short, it is a cleverly designed residence that has grand rooms but few of the pretensions of its Manhattan counterparts.

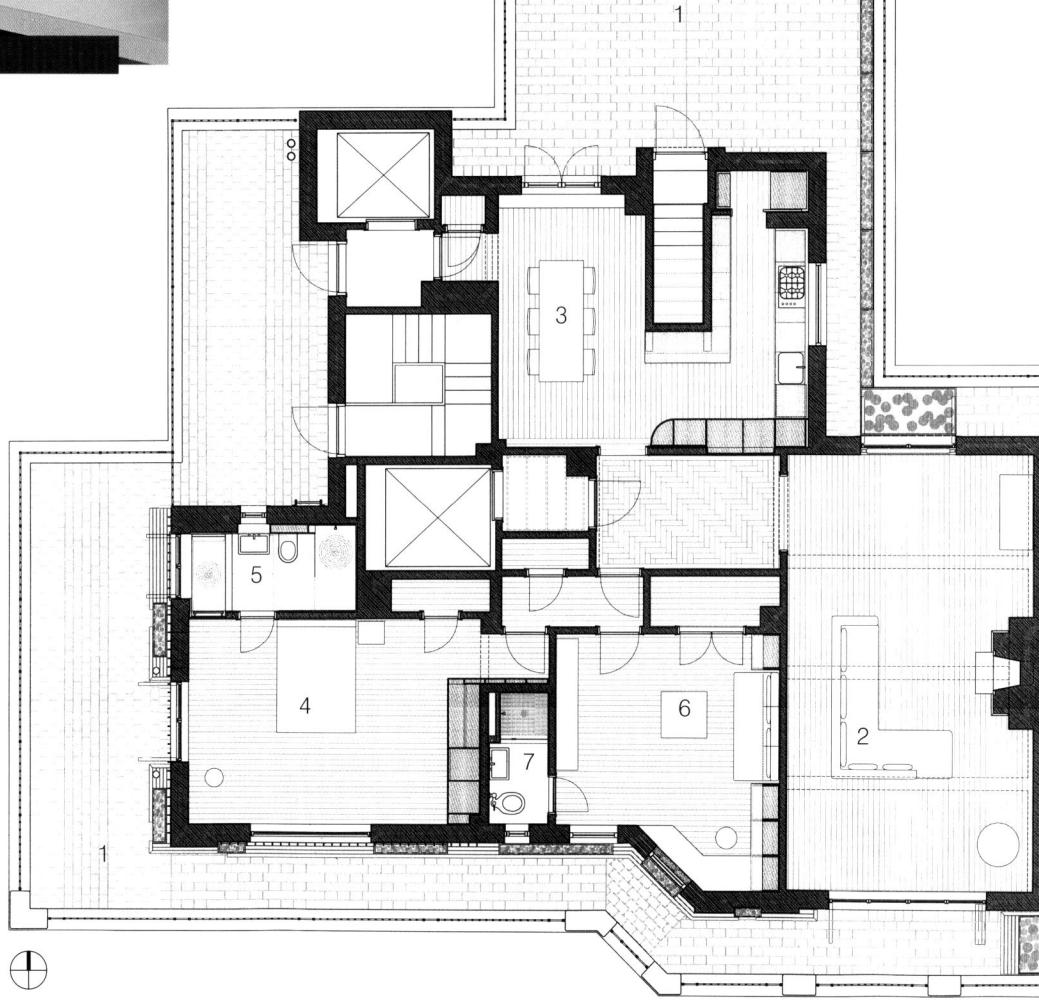

1 Terrace
2 Living room
3 Kitchen/dining
4 Bedroom
5 Bathroom
6 Bedroom/study
7 Bathroom

terrace theater

Rome, Italy
Studio Transit

There is almost a sense of *trompe l'oeil* about this apartment, located at the top level of an ancient palazzo high above the rooftops of Rome. Walls feature decorative effects and faux finishes to create a fantastic illusion, while stairs appear out of nowhere and then disappear again, almost as if on a stage. Even the reflections of the white clouds and blue sky in the windows of the bathroom, which has a bird's eye view of the startlingly beautiful horizon, seem surreal, as if they've been painted on by an enthusiastic designer inspired by an Italian master. And up on the terrace, which is surrounded by orange trees and the enchanting rooftops of Rome, the setting of chairs and a dining table placed gently amid the serenity is simply magic.

Designed by architect Danilo Parisio, the two-floor apartment is testament to what can be achieved with little space but lots of effort. Parisio, a demanding perfectionist, wanted to decorate his private domain with the same meticulous approach he applies to his clients' dwellings while creating a showpiece of everything he considers of primary importance in modern-day homes, namely theatre and setting, landscape and view. "The right blend of atmosphere and function is integral in interiors," he says, "and the right balance must be found before planning any living space." Parisio knew he wanted to design an inspirational retreat in the heart of Rome; a place to come home to and relax in at the end of a day, and so he set about creating a mix of reality and fantasy, or functionality and fabulousness. The terrace helped, of course, offering a place to pour a wine among the rooftops of the city, right in front of the steeple of Santa Maria, and entertain and enthrall guests with the drama of it all, but there were also other elements that added to the apartment's spectacle and thrill. Mirrors were one, offering illusion and light throughout the space, and enlarging spaces while making visual 'cuts' in other places that would be otherwise structurally impossible to break. Windows were another design trick, allowing light to flow through generously sized glass while framing the memorable view. Full height glazed doors also highlighted Rome's most beautiful sights, while adding to the illusion of 'grandness'.

The first floor was given over to principal rooms—a central lobby, a kitchen, a dining room, and a spacious living room opening to the elongated terrace. A lean staircase lined in natural stone was created to lead to the second level, where a master bedroom with an ensuite and a smaller guest bedroom were set. But while each of the rooms have their impressive merits, it is the tiny ensuite that really shines in the apartment's design. Furnished with a Jacuzzi tub, it opens to a small, secluded terrace, where bathers can escape to dry off in the sun. Truly a private space in the bustling heart of Rome.

tower
spectacle

Melbourne, Victoria, Australia
Rori Homes

Situated on level 27 of an apartment tower in Melbourne's inner-city Southbank precinct, this penthouse offers spectacular views over the city, Port Phillip Bay and Albert Park Lake, site of the Formula One Australian Grand Prix. The challenge was to create an interior that would be as impressive as the vista it looked out over, although the owner brought to the table many of his own design ideas, having been inspired by the grandeur of penthouses in places like Dubai.

The open-plan interior was created from the merger of two neighboring apartments and the amalgamation resulted in a lavish floor plan that features five bathrooms, three spacious bedrooms (including a principal suite with a built-in library and his-and-hers bathrooms), an entrance hall, a gymnasium, and an entertainment area with a commercial-size bar. There is also a separate office with its own boardroom, plus four outdoor balconies for alfresco entertaining.

Two laser-cut, rust-coated wall features were imported from China for the formal lounge, while Wandoo timber recycled from a 100-year-old wool storage shed in Western Australia was used for the floor of the bar area. These 'rustic' surfaces were the perfect backdrop for the cutting-edge technology that was incorporated into much of the interior, blending old and new together in a curiously symbiotic fit. As befitting a modern penthouse, the techno-gadgets include portable touch pads enabling remote control from any room, an elaborate fiber-optics lighting system that changes the color of the bar depending on the mood required, and a drop-down LCD screen, along with nine televisions and 20 built-in speakers.

Topped off with a baby grand piano, set theatrically against a stunning city skyline backdrop, the apartment is a perfect play area high above the hustle and bustle of the city.

venetian dreams

Venice, Italy
Filippa Gaggia

Surrounded on three sides by shimmering bodies of water—St. Mark's Basin, the Giudecca Canal, and the Grand Canal—the Dorsoduro is perhaps the most beautiful neighborhood in Venice. Reached by boat or foot (via the Ponte dell'Accademia, an enchanting wooden bridge spanning the Grand Canal), this quarter of the city is defined by its dramatic Baroque skyline, its narrow canals, and its charming walled gardens. It is also the preferred hangout for artists, designers, and writers attracted by the light, the architecture, and of course the views. Peggy Guggenheim, the American heiress and art patron, famously settled here in a waterfront palace, while other residents, including the Marchesa Luisa Casati, who had a penchant for pet cheetahs and gold-leafed houseboys, added their own eclectic personalities to the place.

Such is the theater and spectacle of this magic corner of Venice that in recent years, it has become an in-demand area for hoteliers and wealthy Venetians to renovate grand, centuries-old buildings and transform them into stylish, restorative retreats, of which this villa is a superb example.

Located in a grand building overlooking the overlooking the Rio di San Barnaba, with the nearest vaporetto stop being the Ca' Rezzonico, the duplex apartment has its own private terrace and garden—a rarity in Venice. Outside, the architecture is classic Venice: slightly worn but still grand. Inside, the interior is pure luxury. Renovated to a high standard with modern materials and clever features, the apartment's new design is unexpectedly edgy, while still offering character, light, and traditional Venetian charm.

The principal rooms consist of two kitchens, two living areas—one upstairs and another downstairs—and a magical dining room fronting the canal, which offers a space to entertain against the theater of the city. This space extends out to a terrace, which provides another spot to sit and pour a fine wine as the sun sinks over the famous canals. A Steinway piano adds sound to the setting, as if it wasn't soaked in glamour enough already.

There is also a garden, enclosed on three sides—a delightfully shady place to escape the heat in the middle of the day.

It is a true oasis in the heart of the city: a modern, but timeless sanctuary filled with fine design and pleasing lines. Just like the city itself.

Photography: Manuel Zoblena

view to a thrill

Columbus, Ohio, USA
Gwathmey Siegel & Associates Architects

Columbus isn't the first city that comes to mind when you think of penthouses and views. But this extraordinary apartment proves that you can have eye-catching vistas anywhere.

Located on the top floor of an apartment building in downtown Columbus, adjacent to the river with panoramic views, it was always going to be a spectacular place to live. But when Gwathmey Siegel & Associates Architects received the commission to transform it into a luxury retreat, the potential for it to be a truly amazing home went through the penthouse roof.

Already enhanced by light and scale, the apartment was reconfigured to allow for the views—both those of the city and river, and those of the owner's major modern art collection. The program specified a library and private office suite, a living area, a formal dining space, a kitchen/dining/family room, an exercise space and spa, a master bedroom suite, three guest bedroom suites, a sculpture terrace and, finally, a gallery. The sculpture terrace in itself was a challenge, but organizing the floor plan around the oversized pieces of art required some deft thinking. The solution was to design a gallery space that not only showcased the art but also separated the double-height living volumes, with their views, from the service spaces and building cores. This entry gallery, accessed from the north elevator lobby, opens to the sculpture terrace and encourages the flow to the family spaces, which are revealed sequentially.

In addition to this, a 100-foot-long wedge-shaped triangular skylight releases the roof to the sky and floods this grand interior with natural light, balancing the two-story glass perimeter walls, and adding a dynamic, volumetric, referential, and almost iconic form to the space.

The second level, accessed by two stairs, one from the living and the other from the family room, accommodates the master bedroom suite, with its balcony terrace overlooking the city and river, and a guest bedroom suite, with a balcony sitting area over the library. The counterpoint between wall and glass, solid and void, establishes a dynamic and hierarchical layering of space, which is simultaneously enriched and reinforced by the integration of the art collection into the architecture.

window on the world

New York, New York, USA

Resolution: 4 Architecture

When it came to his home, architect Peter Eisenman decided to employ the services of renowned New York firm Resolution: 4 Architecture to update his Manhattan apartment and make it more livable for him and his family. The 2000-square-foot apartment is located in a residential tower that gazes out over lower Manhattan. Views are in abundance here, but it is the artwork and books that really catch visitors' eyes when they first walk in. As much a part of the home as its design, these books and art pieces make up an extensive and varied collection, collected from global journeys over the years, and are very dear to the family's heart. Thus, they were first on the list of priorities for the Resolution: 4 architects, who were briefed to provide plenty of space for not only these but also future purchases.

The main challenge was combining these pieces with a functional floor plan designed for family living, while opening up the space to its incredible views. The solution was to reconfigure the interior around a series of three distinct ceiling heights and an overlapping design of public and private zones. By manipulating the relationship between the floor and ceiling plates, a new spatial ordering system emerges, which frames the horizon by compressing the interior space. The variance not only modulates the apartment's interior volumes but also allows the interior to flow out toward the spectacular urban scene that spreads from its windows. The overlapping design, meanwhile, gives the residence a new flexibility, so that rooms can offer more than one function: an integral part of life in New York where space is at a premium.

The new design allows three bedroom areas to revolve around a kitchen, a living space, and a library, so that the floor plan is easy to navigate, but also allows private spaces for family members to retreat to. From the entry, the home opens laterally to the library/study on one side and a living area on the other. Beyond these rooms there is a guest closet and bathroom, and at the link between public and private spaces, an eat-in kitchen where the family can gravitate to in order to chat and catch up at the end of the day. A rolling breakfast table allows easy access to a built-in bench, but it can also roll into the living area to extend the library table for dinner parties.

It is a neat, streamlined, highly tailored space that accommodates a busy family while providing an inspirational outlook over the city. The perfect home for an architect and his family.

index

aardvarchitecture, New York, USA
terrace for two   164
www.aardvarchi.com

Abode, Sydney, Australia
sydney vista   156
www.abodeint.com.au

Alex Mony, Paris, France
paris match   116
paris perfect   122
a sense of place   142
www.parisvacationapartments.com

Archiforma, Miami, USA
miami glamor   104
www.archiformagroup.com
www.majesticproperties.com

Axis Mundi and Studio ST, New York, USA
duplex for a gentleman   38
www.axismundi.com
www.studio-st.com

Claudio Silvestrin, London, UK
simple luxuries   148
www.claudiosilvestrin.com

DS Architecture, New York, USA
box seat   14
www.dsarchitecture.com

Filippa Gaggia, Venice, Italy
venetian dreams   182
www.viewsonvenice.com

Foley & Cox, New York, USA
duplex drama   32
www.foleyandcox.com

Form Design Architecture, London, UK
living large in london   84
www.form-architecture.co.uk

Greg Natale Interior Design, Sydney, Australia
haute couture on the harbor   60
www.gregnatale.com

Gwathmey Siegel & Associates Architects, New York, USA
central park art   20
fifth avenue   44
view to a thrill   190
www.gwathmey-siegel.com

Hariri & Hariri, New York, USA
grey scale   54
www.haririandhariri.com

James Swan & Company, Los Angeles, USA
la luxe   78
www.jamesswanco.com

Janson Goldstein, New York, USA
fine lines   48
www.jansongoldstein.com

lazzarini pickering architetti, Rome, Italy
pure positano   128
www.lazzarinipickering.com

Louise Braverman, New York, USA
new york, new york   110
www.newyork-architects/louise.braverman

Resolution: 4 Architecture, New York, USA
loft for a super hero   90
window on the world   194
www.re4a.com

Rori Homes, Melbourne, Australia
tower spectacle   174
www.rorihomes.com.au

Silvestri Architettura, Genoa, Italy
la dolce vita   70
www.silvestri.info

Smith-Miller + Hawkinson Architects, New York, USA
manhattan transfer   98
www.smharch.com

Studio Gaia, New York, USA
cream of the crop   26
www.studiogaia.com

Studio Transit, Rome, Italy
roman holiday   136
terrace theater   170
www.studiotransit.it

Wood Marsh and Mirvac, Melbourne, Australia
high life   64
www.woodmarsh.com.au
www.mirvac.com.au

30 – 39

20 – 29

10 – 19

GR – 9

BASEMENT